WOODCARVING
10 ORIGINAL PROJECTS

Woodcarving

Jeremy Williams

The Crowood Press

First published in 1996 by
The Crowood Press Ltd
Ramsbury, Marlborough
Wiltshire SN8 2HR

British Library Cataloguing-in-Publication Data
A catalogue record for this book is available from the British Library.

ISBN 1 85223 926 3

Picture Credits
All photographs by David Scholes.
Line-drawings by Bob Constant.

Typeset by Footnote Graphics, Warminster, Wiltshire.
Printed and bound by BPC Consumer Books Ltd, Aylesbury

Contents

Acknowledgements

During the course of writing this book I have received assistance from a number of sources.

I should like to express my thanks to Henry Taylor (Tools) Limited for their help and advice; for their permission to reproduce the chart of carving tool shapes and sizes; and not least for making such fine tools that last for years and years. I bought my first Henry Taylor gouges nearly fifty years ago and I still use them.

I am indebted to Geoff Jackson of Lizard Designs for the loan of the extra workholder.

My thanks are also due to photographer David Scholes for all the hard work he put in taking the pictures used in this book.

To John Bradford, of Wiggaton, Devon, and to Steve Collett of Cornish Woodcrafts, for selling me such good quality timber – a pleasure to use. To my good neighbours Ian Cox and Alan Pearce of Rozen Furniture, my thanks for helping out by planing and trimming wood for me. A thank you is also due to Nick Haslam of CSM Trade Supplies for information relating to Hermes Abrasives.

My thanks, also, to my carving friends, and students past and present, for their comments and opinions, which I sought when the projects were being planned and which I found so useful.

And, not least of all, my thanks to my wife, Jeane, for putting up with my constant 'chip-chatter' over the last few months.

Finally, I should like to thank those people who have kindly given me help in the preparation of this book, whose names I have failed to mention.

Introduction

For some time I have felt there is a need for a book of woodcarving projects. In writing it I have drawn on both my experience of teaching woodcarving during the last twelve years, as well as on some of the things I have learnt in over forty years of playing about with wood. While teaching I have found that it is not at all uncommon for beginners to need a guiding hand to help them gain the confidence to work on their own. In this book I have tried to do this. This book is not intended only for the complete novice, however; those recently new to the craft, who seldom seem to have time spare to delve into researching ideas of their own, will, I hope, find the projects useful.

For those who have yet to know something of the pleasure of working wood with hand-tools, I have felt it desirable to include some basic facts about tools, timber, design and safety. I hope readers who already carve – and know there can be heartache as well as pleasure in fashioning wood – will find some of the facts I have mentioned worth their reading, or dare I say re-learning.

I have arranged the subjects so that the projects follow on from each other, progressively, along a logical learning curve. In simple terms this means not trying to run before you have learnt to walk – not an uncommon practice in many classes!

My philosophy has always been 'Start with something simple. Once you have made a start, you will soon begin to build up confidence. What seemed difficult before you started will then become possible.'

All the actual carving of the projects only requires using normal woodcarving tools. In the early stages of construction I may well have used mechanical aids – a bandsaw or a jigsaw, for example, but I have tried to include mention of possible cheaper options for a beginner to buy. Where other general woodwork hand-tools have been used they have been mentioned. I have purposely avoided using rotary cutters, or cutter burrs, even when they could have been an advantage, not because I particularly dislike them, but because I would not wish any reader to feel they have to buy more equipment than is really necessary. After all, a golf bag full of clubs does not make a scratch player!

The scheme of work covers:

• Creating an upright three-dimensional form.
• A three-dimensional horizontal carving.

These are followed by:

• Three projects dealing with movement.

• Decorative work is catered for with projects that use the three main methods – **incised**, **low** and **high relief**; with a separate project on carving a mirror frame.
• The final project deals with the all-important matter of **composition**. It draws on the earlier projects for reference.

For good measure, the sculpture projects and those on decorative carving are interspersed with methods of achieving a good finish to your work.

Woodcarving, like all other art forms, relies greatly on personal interpretation of the subject. And while a novice carver may be quite content to follow my designs faithfully, since his or her need will be to learn technique rather than anything else, others with some experience may wish to make changes to fit in with how they personally visualize the subject. Feel free to do so.

Lastly, there are a couple of points which I would like to bring to your attention. These days, one never really knows if metric measurement is more favoured, or whether a reader is more conversant with the imperial form. I have opted to use both, but where I have felt it appropriate I have not always quoted the precise metric conversion figure, but have stated what I feel to be one more convenient to use. For example, whilst 13mm may be the equivalent of half an inch, in some cases a figure of 10mm might be more readily used.

The second point relates to the working drawings. Every care has been exercised in checking their accuracy. However, production methods, the enlargement or reduction by photocopier, which may be carried out before you use them, can cause some distortion. Be warned: when you start cutting wood, give yourself some margin to spare. Then you should avoid being disappointed.

If this book helps you to take up woodcarving, if it enables you to progress, or if it just acts as a means of re-awakening your interest, it will have done its job. Good luck!

1

Starting Woodcarving

CHOOSING TOOLS

Like most hobbies, before you can start you will need to spend some cash on equipment. Fortunately, though, woodcarving tools last for many years, so what you spend should, providing you have chosen wisely, be around for a very long time. People sometimes ask if there is any merit in buying second-hand. Well, there are those who claim that the tools of yesteryear are sounder than those of recent manufacture. There may be some truth in this, especially as far as tiny tools used for decorative work are concerned, though good examples are getting harder to find. But there are certainly very good new tools being made these days. The majority of beginners probably end up buying new, and in many ways this is not such a bad thing. It permits individual selection to be made to suit one's personal requirements, providing you

know what you want, rather than having to take over sizes and shapes chosen by somebody else years ago. So, with this in mind, let us start by looking at carving tools, and what you need to take into account when making a selection, as well as some of the other bits and pieces needed to start carving.

The Shapes of Carving Tools (Fig 1)

If you look at a manufacturer's catalogue you will find a bewildering range of carving tools, numbering in excess of one and a half thousand if all the variables of size and shape are added together. To any beginner this can be mind-boggling. Why do there have to be so many shapes and sizes? It can all get quite confusing, but in fact it is really all very straightforward.

When viewed end-on, carving tools fall into two

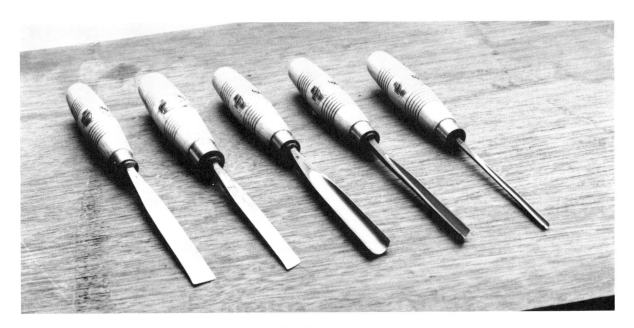

Fig 2   No. 1 and No. 2 chisels, No. 9 gouge, V-tool, and No. 11 veiner.

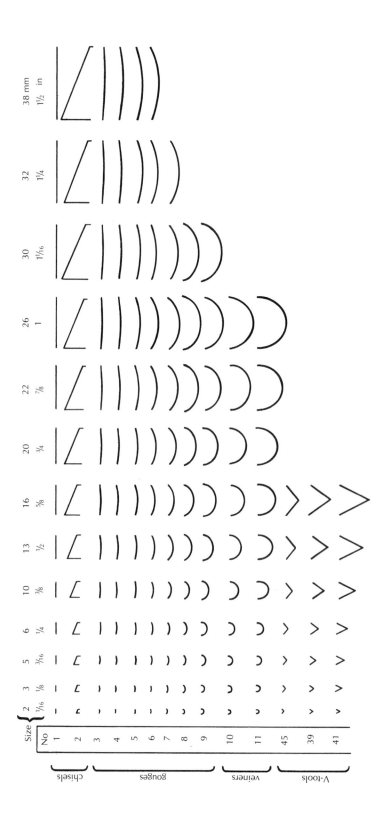

Fig 1 Shapes of woodcarving tools, by courtesy of Henry Taylor (Tools) Ltd.

basic categories. There are the **chisels** which have flat blades, and with ends either ground straight across, or on a skew; and there are **gouges**. These are the ones which, when you look at their tips, are curved. This curve is known as the **sweep** of the gouge. As you can see from the chart, the sweep can vary from a shallow to a steep U-shape. There are other types which are not rounded, but V-shaped. These are known as **V-tools**, or **parting tools**. Gouges make up the greater part of the range of woodcarving tools.

Blade Shapes (Fig 2)

The majority of carving tools used, irrespective of whether they are chisels or gouges, have blades with straight sides when viewed from above (as shown in the photograph). To cope with specific needs, for improved visibility, or for working in confined spaces, other shapes evolved. Of these the more common types are:

• **Fishtail   (Fig 3)**   This shape allows you to see better when cutting but, owing to its slender shaft, the tool is never as strong as a conventional gouge. Fishtails are ideal for making light, finishing cuts. When the blade is drawn back less steeply, they are known as a **longpods**.

Fig 3   Fishtail gouge.

• **Curved or Salmon Bent   (Fig 4)**   This shape is ideal for cutting down into a shallow depression.

Fig 4   Curved, or salmon bent gouge.

• **Spoon-Shaped Gouges   (Fig 5)**   Mainly used in decorative work, but also occasionally in sculpture. The front-bent types (a) scoop deeper than curved gouges. They can also be used when part of a design obstructs or hinders the entry of straight-bladed gouges. Back-bent gouges (b) can be used to groove a convex-curved shape.

(a)

(b)

Fig 5   Spoon-shaped gouges, (a) Front bent (b) Back bent

• **Dog-Leg Chisel   (Fig 6)**   This tool works in a similar way to a spoon gouge. The blade shaft is cranked to allow cuts, which might otherwise be hindered by an existing part of the design.

Fig 6   Dog-leg chisel.

• **Allongee Shape   (Fig 7)**   Very wide gouges with straight sides would clearly be cumbersome to manipulate, but to be strong they cannot be of the fishtail pattern. Usually, then, they have tapering sides and are known as allongee types. Their disadvantage is that, like the fishtails, the more they are sharpened the narrower the cutting edge becomes. This is why the allongee shape is not particularly popular.

Fig 7   Allongee shape.

The Numbering System

Gouges and chisels are identified by a number which is usually stamped on the blade. The numbers are based on what is known as the Sheffield List. This list was drawn up a hundred years or more ago to standardize tool shapes. But, like so many rules and regulations, the idea while fine in theory falls a little short in practice. No two manufacturers will ever produce identical gouge shapes. This, though, is not a reflection on their tool-making ability. It is brought about by the fact that good carving tools are still forged by hand, and manufacturing tolerances must be expected. Variation of sweep, from one make to another, is bound to occur.

This does not matter when you are actually carving, for you will only be concerned with your own tools, and you will know their shapes whatever their make. But it can cause minor problems if you read about carving and do not know the brand the writer uses. There are differences amongst some English makes, and between European makes and English patterns. This applies especially to the shallower cuts. For example, an English No. 3 gouge is slightly steeper than a Swiss No. 3. To make things easy,

throughout this book the numbers mentioned are those applicable to the gouges made by the old established firm Henry Taylor (Tools) Limited of Sheffield, England, and the shapes of the sweeps illustrated are theirs.

Gouge Numbers (Fig 8)

For straight blades, gouge numbering starts at No. 3, with No. 1 and No. 2 being reserved for chisels (No. 1 when ground straight across the edge, and No. 2 when set askew).

Run your eye down the shapes. Note how the numbers ascend as the sweeps get steeper. The sweeps relate to the possible depth of cut. A No. 3 gouge has a shallow cut, but a No. 9, which has a semi-circular shape, will cut deeply. It is often called a 'quick-cut' gouge.

With gouges No. 10 and No. 11 the sides of the blade are drawn up. They have become **U**-shaped. One of the uses of this type is to cut decorative lines. The wider versions will cut deep flutes; the smaller ones, still known by their archaic name **veiners**, will cut leaf veins.

V-shaped tools come in three angles: 90 degrees (type 45), 45 degrees (type 39) and 60 degrees (type 41). The 45-degree ones are popular, but I prefer the 60-degree setting. For the projects in this book, either a no. 39 or a no. 41 can be used.

All manufacturers have to be able to differentiate between straight-blade gouges and other blade shapes. Again, the Sheffield List is used. For example, a shallow spoon gouge is numbered 24 although its sweep is the same as a No. 3 straight gouge. Manufacturers may add extra numbers of their own. In the Henry Taylor series, the No. 24 spoon is designated a No. 3724.

Size of Tools

The size of the tools used is very much controlled by the scale of the carving being undertaken. This does not necessarily mean you have to have a vast array of gouges and chisels to become an adept carver. You can use the same gouge for various sizes of work. In all probability much of your early sculpture will be using timber roughly the size of a house brick, and relief carvings will be about A4 or A3 paper size. As a guide, tools ranging from $\frac{1}{8}$in (3mm) up to $\frac{3}{4}$in (20mm) will cover your needs.

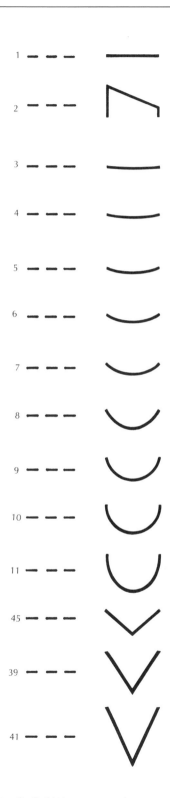

Fig 8   *Sheffield List gouge numbers.*

SELECTING CARVING TOOLS

The truth is that in fact only a modest number are needed to start with. Eventually you are sure to want to expand the range, as this will help to extend your repertoire of style. But do not be tempted to buy too many gouges at the outset; gain some practical experience first. Those shown in bold type in the following list are all you will probably need. Certainly you should avoid boxed sets, for invariably there will be at least one gouge, or chisel, you will never, ever use, meaning a waste of money.

And finally, try and persuade your family not to rush out and buy tools for you when they know you are thinking of taking up carving. I have seen it happen time and time again, when teaching. A student arrives with the most horrendous set of tools, saying:

'I was given these the other day by my wife/husband/son/daughter. Are they any good?'

That really does require a diplomatic answer!

The Types Chosen

With cost in mind, selection has been divided into two parts – those gouges and chisels regarded as essential, in bold type, and optional ones. Generally speaking, decorative carving requires more shapes and sizes than are needed for sculpture. To simplify matters I have indicated the actual gouges used to carve each of the projects. They have been taken from this list.

Chisels	Gouges
½in (13mm) No. 1	**¼in (6mm) No. 3**
⅜in (10mm) No. 2 Skew	½in (13mm) No. 3 Fishtail
¼in (6mm) Dog-Leg No. 1	¾in (20mm) No. 3
	¾in (20mm) No. 4
	¼in (6mm) No. 6 Longpod
	¾in (20mm) No. 5
	½in (13mm) No. 6
	³⁄₁₆in (5mm) No. 7
	½in (13mm) No. 7
	¼in (6mm) No. 9
	½in (13mm) No. 9
	⅛in (3mm) No. 11
	³⁄₁₆in (5mm) No. 11
	¼in (6mm) No. 41 V-tool

CARING FOR YOUR TOOLS

Firstly, make sure you have the means to store your carving tools so they do not get damaged. Hanging gouges on the workshop wall may seem a great idea, they look good, but they can get rusty. It is far better to keep them in a canvas tool-roll. Aim to buy one that has twelve pockets, with your first tool purchase. As your range increases you may need to think in terms of a specially made cabinet with individual compartments, but this will not be for some time.

OTHER TOOLS

Other tools, beside gouges and chisels, will be needed. Probably the most important will be those that will keep your carving tools razor-sharp. These are dealt with in the next chapter, which covers the basics of sharpening.

Some tools, like handsaws and wood rasps, you may have already; perhaps even power equipment, such as a bandsaw or a router. If you do not have any tools of your own, ask around. Woodworkers are generally friendly people, and only too happy to lend a helping hand to somebody new to the craft. It may not be necessary to spend a fortune on equipment

just to get started. That can come later, when you are selling your work!

Instead of being listed here, you will find various tools introduced in the project chapters. There are, however, one or two specific items worth mentioning now.

• **Carver's Mallet (Fig 9)** As shown in the photograph, this is short and stubby, with a round head that does not deflect the path of a gouge, as a square head would do when hit off-centre.

Mallets are made in different weights and sizes, either from Beech, or from a dense wood like Lignum vitae, which is now becoming rare. Choose one of about 3in (75mm) in diameter. Many people seem to get on better with the slightly heavier Lignum type, but others prefer to use a Beech one, knowing that the wood is sustainable.

• **Workbench (Fig 10)** Carving needs to be carried out on a robust bench, or on a strong table. If starting from scratch, then it will be worth your while making a workbench to suit your exact requirements. This particularly applies to the working height, for there is nothing worse than having to stoop to carve. Generally, the standard height of a carpentry bench is too low. If you construct your own, or have one

Fig 9 Carver's mallet.

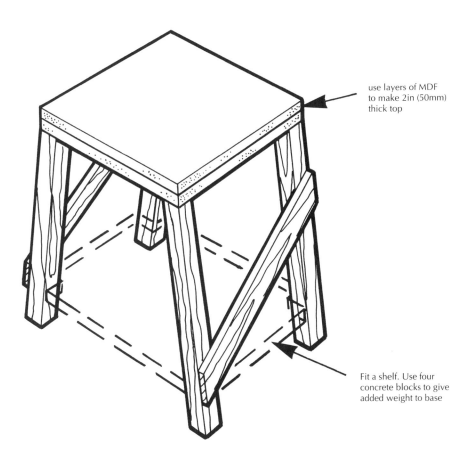

use layers of MDF
to make 2in (50mm)
thick top

Fit a shelf. Use four
concrete blocks to give
added weight to base

Fig 10   Carver's workbench.

made for you, think in terms of it being 34–36in (865–915mm) high, if you are of average height, and with a top of about 20in (500mm) square. Use stout timber for the frame.

● **Workholding (Figs 11 and 12)** Some form of workholder for sculpture will be required. Often, workholders are also suitable for holding relief carvings. Standard woodwork vices can be used, but this usually entails fixing the carving block to a shaped piece of wood, so that it can be rotated to allow all-round carving to be carried out. There are purpose-made carving vices and, as you would expect, they come in a fairly wide price range. The swivelling types allow the work to be positioned as needed, which means the carver does not have to be a contortionist!

Fig 11   A workholder.
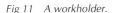

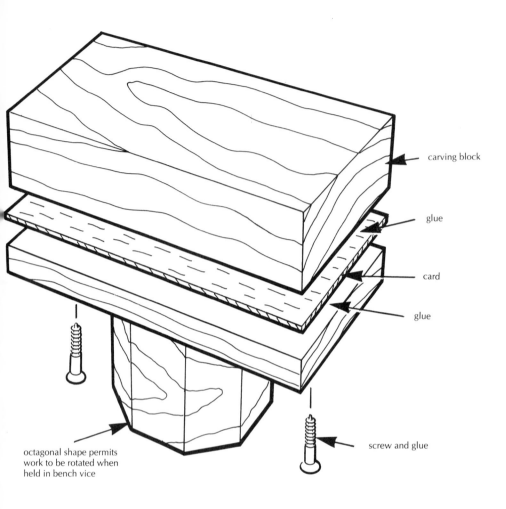

carving block

glue

card

glue

screw and glue

octagonal shape permits
work to be rotated when
held in bench vice

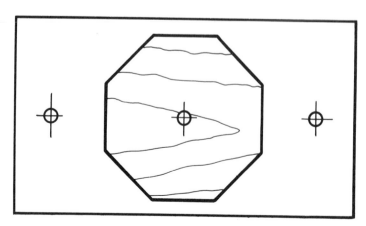

use only centre stem for small blocks

Fig 12   Suitable support for carving blocks.

2

Tool Sharpening

TOOLS MUST BE RAZOR-SHARP

The creation of a successful woodcarving can prove to be very enjoyable. It is certainly a wonderful feeling to slice with relative ease through the wood, and to leave a bright and crisply cut surface. But these things are only ever possible if the gouges and chisels being used are razor-sharp.

While it is possible to buy carving tools which have been factory sharpened, do remember that, with use, any tool will soon begin to become blunt. So, some basic knowledge of how to sharpen carving tools is essential.

The Link between Sharpening and Good Workmanship

Maintaining really sharp cutting edges is so part and parcel of woodcarving that it should never be considered a chore to be carried out only infrequently. The act of sharpening should be an ongoing task, requiring only a few moments of time, to restore a cutting edge to pristine condition. With experience, you will begin to sense, simply by how the tool is working, that it is losing a little of its sharpness. You will also know, again from experience, that to attend to its restoration then will only necessitate a few honing strokes. If left unattended, the blunting will get progressively worse, and it will become harder and harder to cut the wood. Bits may even start to break off or split, and the end result is more likely to be one of sheer frustration than pure enjoyment – when you think about it, this is not very surprising: few people would attempt to use a blunt knife to sharpen a pencil, or to slice bread; they would soon do something about it – by sharpening the knife, or maybe these days, by buying a new, disposable one. When it comes to carving wood, it is surprising just how many students try to battle away with blunt tools, or with incorrectly set cutting edges.

THE DYNAMICS OF SHARPENING

Anyone seriously wishing to progress needs fully to understand the mechanics of tool sharpening, and the geometry of cutting edges. They are fundamental to good carving practice. The basic facts are not difficult to grasp, and it may be useful to highlight the main points here.

Bevel Angles (Fig 13)

During manufacture, the thickness of the steel forming a blade is tapered to form the cutting edge by grinding. This is known as the **bevel**.

These days, most makes of carving tools have factory-ground bevels set, on the outside of the blade, at between 20 and 25 degrees; and most people are content to go along with the angles chosen by the manufacturer. Two points are, however, worth remembering:

Firstly, the shallower the bevel, the thinner the steel close to the cutting edge, and the weaker the blade tip becomes, even when properly forged and hardened. If used to carve a wood which is very hard, some damage to the cutting edge may occur. Additional strength, meaning a steeper bevel angle, could then be an advantage. So remember, the angle of a bevel is arbitrary. It can be adjusted to suit the nature of the wood.

Secondly, the set of a bevel is linked to the force needed to drive the gouge into the wood. A shallow bevel requires less effort than one set at a steep angle. Consequently, low-angle bevels are best for shallow cuts, often powered by hand pressure. But steeper bevels may be required when energetic removal of tough wood is carried out.

Sharpening Stones

Gouges and chisels may be sharpened using bench-stones. These abrasive stones, natural or man-made,

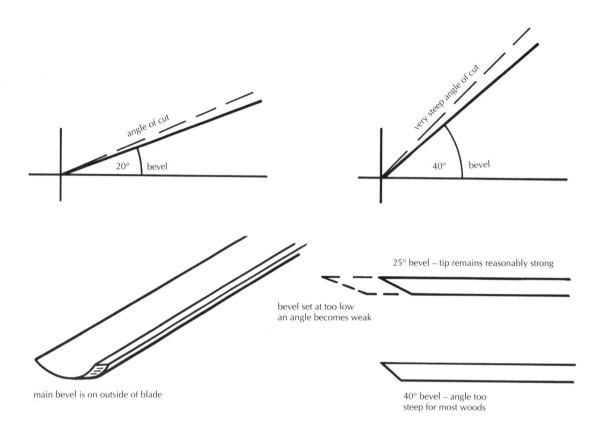

Fig 13   Bevel angles.

are lubricated with oil or with water, depending on which type they are. I prefer to use oilstones. These are natural Arkansas stones or the man-made 'India' types. Personally, I find waterstones – the ones lubricated with water – too soft, although many carvers do like them. Stones come in various grades from coarse to very fine. Each can be of a single grade, or it can combine two different grades, for example, coarse on one side; medium grade on the other. A good choice is a combination stone – man-made coarse/medium – and a separate natural single grade fine stone. Keep one side of a single stone for gouges, as these eventually groove the surface, and keep the other side flat for sharpening chisels. Stones are best kept in wooden boxes. Oilstones are lubricated with light oil.

Avoid Bevel Wobble (Fig 14)

The bevel of the blade has to be kept in contact with the stone, *always at the same angle*. It should not be allowed to wobble. It is usual to work across the stone when sharpening a gouge, and along the stone's length for a chisel. Note that a carver's chisel is bevelled on both sides of the blade. Work each side, counting the number of strokes, to maintain equal bevels.

A wrist-twisting action is needed to sharpen a gouge. This will ensure that all the **sweep** comes into contact with the surface of the stone. But it is essential to ensure this action is neither exaggerated, nor diminished, as in either case a faulty cutting edge will then be the result.

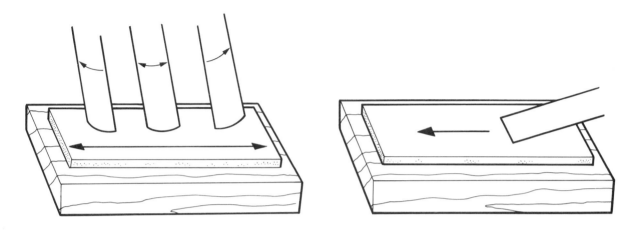

Fig 14 (a) Gouge honing sequence – arrows on blades show direction of twist. Arrow on oilstone indicates gouge travel across oilstone. (b) Chisel blade moves in one direction.

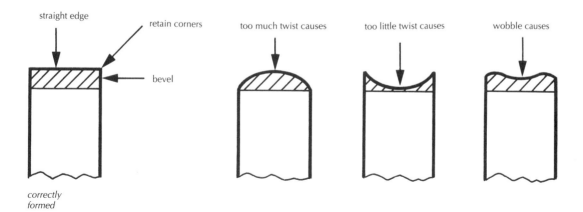

Fig 15 Common results of faulty sharpening.

Avoid a Rounded Bevel (Figs 16–20)

This is also caused by wobbling during sharpening. It is vital that the length of the bevel face remains as flat as possible. The way the gouge is held is important.

Figs 17 and 18 show how to hold a gouge right-handedly. By keeping the right wrist and forearm in line with each other, blade wobble is minimized. Work from side to side to sharpen a gouge, Fig 19, and along the stone's length for a chisel, Fig 20.

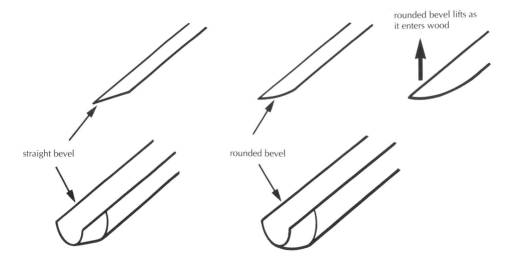

Fig 16   Straight and rounded bevels. Rounded bevel lifts as it starts cutting.

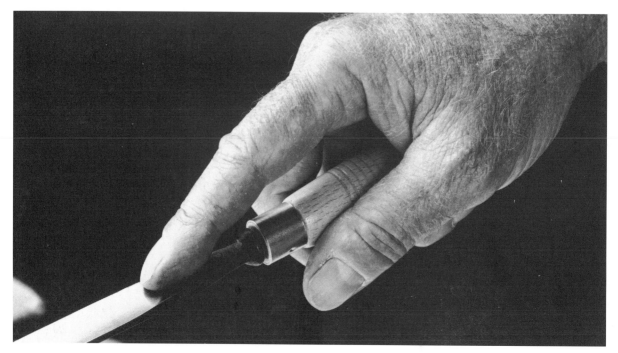

Fig 17   Gouge sharpening, showing right-hand position when holding tool.

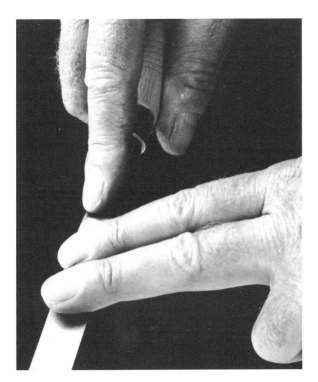

Fig 18   Gouge sharpening: position of left fingers.

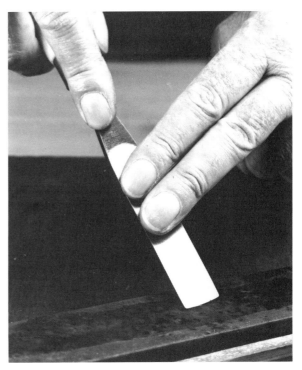

Fig 19   Honing a gouge.

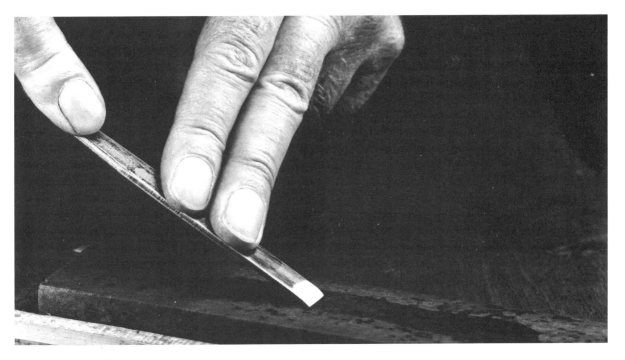

Fig 20   Honing a chisel.

Slipstones (Figs 21–23)

When a tool is sharpened to its edge, the very last part of the steel forming the bevel turns over and forms a roughness, known as the **burr**, on the inside of the blade. The burr is removed with a small, shaped stone called a **slipstone**. They come in a variety of sizes to match different gouge sweeps, and are made from the same material as the oilstones. Slipstones can be used to form a small bevel on the inside edge of the blade; useful when a gouge is used upside-down.

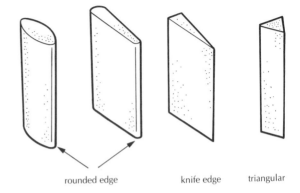

rounded edge   knife edge   triangular

Fig 21   Some slipstones.

Fig 22   Using a slipstone, flat on blade.

Fig 23   Using a slipstone – angled on blade for inside bevel.

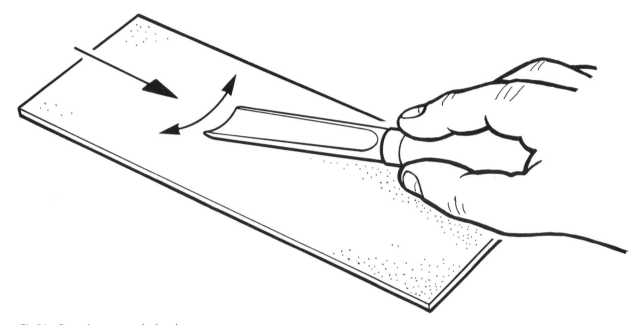

Fig 24   Stropping a gouge by hand.

Stropping (Fig 24)

A very fine cutting edge is maintained if the carving tools are regularly **stropped**. This is done by pulling the cutting edge across a strip of leather. Ideally, the leather should have a rough surface – a nap – and to improve its polishing property it can be coated with a mild abrasive compound like valve grinding paste or chrome polish. If tallow is applied to the leather this will help to keep it supple.

Mechanical Honing (Fig 25)

Another way to sharpen tools, and one which is gaining in popularity, is to use felt or composite wheels attached to an electric motor. The wheels are coated with a mild abrasive wax compound, which polishes the bevel to razor-sharpness. There are a number of systems sold, but they all work in a similar way. Many carvers prefer this method of sharpening to all others.

Fig 25   A rotary honing system.

The Choice of Wood

It is important to select the appropriate wood to suit the carving. If the choice is good, the overall effect will be good and the carving will look right. Choose the wrong wood and you run the risk of being disappointed with the end result, for the overall effect may be poor. So, how do you know the right wood to use?

COLOUR AND FIGURING

A wood with very distinctive figuring – generally known as having a strong grain – can enhance a carving, providing it is in keeping with the scale of the work. But, when the subject is small or delicate it can prove too dominant.

STRUCTURE (Fig 26)

Structure is very important. In some timbers the cells are bonded together, like tightly packed drinking straws. These close-grain woods will take fine detail well. In others, though, the cells may be weakly held in place. Some may lie in layers at an angle to the main run of the grain, known, then, as inter-locked grain. Such types will be better suited for chunky sculpture, or to bold relief work which does not demand fine detail. You can test how easily the cells can be split apart by prising with your thumbnail across a corner. If the wood splits easily, cell bonding is weak, meaning the wood will be unsuitable for any delicate, or detailed work.

TYPES OF TIMBER

Woods fall into two broad categories, depending on rate of growth. Trees that have grown quickly tend to produce fibrous timber unsuitable for carving, whilst slow-growing trees – those with lots of annual rings – provide dense, stable, workable wood. The quick-

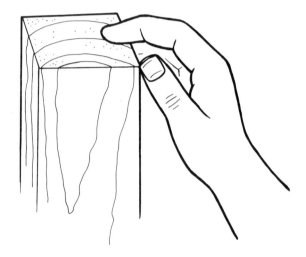

Fig 26   Use your thumbnail to test cell bonding.

growing trees are often of evergreen – or coniferous type – and the slower-growing trees broadleaf or deciduous.

There are many woods used for carving. The following are just some of the most popular ones:

• **Lime**   (*Tilia vulgaris/cordata*). Easy to work. Very close cell structure. Takes detail well. Colour is light and grain seldom distinctive.

• **Sycamore**   (*Acer pseudoplatanus*). A little harder in density than Lime, but having similar small cells. Near white colour with a subtle ripple-pattern grain.

• **Chestnut**   Sweet/Spanish (*Castanea sativa*). Moderately easy to work. Resembles Oak in many respects. Cell structure weak. Grain can often be 'open' giving a coarse look, so not suited to fine detail. Colour is pale brown.

• **Elm**   (*Ulmus* spp). Distinctive, strongly figured, now difficult to find in good quality due to Dutch Elm disease. The coarse but stable grain is good for a bold style. Quite tough to work. Colour ranges from light to dark brown. Wych Elm (*Ulmus glabra*) often has a greenish streak.

• **Cherry** (*Prunus spp*). Like all the fruit woods, this makes excellent carving material. Moderately hard – takes a good finish. Has bold figuring. Tight cell structure. Colour is pinkish-brown, streaked with darker lines, sometimes of a shade of green.

• **Plum** (*Prunus domestica*). Quite easy to work, with an attractive reddish-brown colour. Close grain.

• **Apple** (*Malus sylvestris*). Hard, brittle, usually with a twisted grain. Light to dark brown colour.

• **Pear** (*Pyrus communis*). Moderately hard with a very close grain. Colour is light, but goes pink when seasoned by steaming.

• **Oak** (*Quercus* spp). Fairly hard and somewhat coarse in texture. Better suited to large work, or when durability is important, as it weathers well. Usually light in colour, but when diseased can be brown.

• **Walnut** (*Juglans regia*). Moderately hard, but a delight to carve. Takes detail well, being close grained. English Walnut is dark brown; the more plentiful French variety is lighter in colour.

SEASONING, OR DRYING TIME

Only heartwood is normally used, rather than the sapwood, which is usually too soft and fibrous and can be subject to decay.

Freshly cut wood has to dry before it can be used. This is **seasoning** and can take approximately one year for each inch of thickness. While wood purchased from reputable timber merchants should be fully seasoned and ready to use, it can still be preferable to keep it in a cool, dry place at home for a few weeks so that it can acclimatize. This should lessen the risk of it splitting when you start carving.

Basic Design Techniques

GET TO KNOW THE SUBJECT

Thoroughly research your subject. Make preliminary sketches. Take photographs, using a live model, or even a stuffed one. Get to know what the subject looks like, frontally, from above, from the sides and from behind. When you are carving you will need to 'see' its total image.

Visualization

This means being able to hold the image in your mind as you carve. It is not as difficult as it may first seem, but it does require you to concentrate on the subject. Sketching the shape on the wood helps but, in three-dimensional work particularly, the lines drawn soon get cut away. You need a mental picture; the subject visualization – so if you are carving a cat, think cat; if a bird, think bird. Never carve, and at the same time think of something else, like 'what's for lunch/tea/supper'; it will not work.

CLAY MODELS

Technically called 'maquettes', these can help you to get a design right, without having to spend a lot of time cutting wood, and they are particularly useful when planning a subject in three-dimensional form.

Maquettes can be made from pottery clay, or you can use re-usable modelling clay. Sometimes the model may need to be built around a wire frame – an armature – for support. You can make the frame from aluminium armature wire, or you can save money by using old wire coat hangers. To prevent the wire from cutting through the clay, bind it with strips of cloth or paper tape soaked in wallpaper paste.

The clay can be kept workable if covered with a damp cloth, then placed in a plastic bag.

Use a maquette only as a guide. When you carve the subject you will be working with a different medium, and what may look right in clay may not be the same in wood; so be prepared to make changes.

DRAWING

One of the most common mistakes is to produce drawings without taking into account the actual size of the wood to be used.

It is not unusual to hear the complaint, 'the wood isn't really big enough', or 'the carving is too slim.' In actual fact, what the person means is that the design was drawn, then he or she tried to find the right piece of wood and did not quite make it. So, before starting to draw out the design, select the wood.

Width of Wood

Avoid making the mistake of not paying sufficient attention to the *width*. In many cases, the width should be about two-thirds of the subject's length. Relate this to the width of the wood you plan to use, then decide on the length. If you make a habit of setting out like this, you will avoid making carvings too slim. In most three-dimensional work, the back-to-front depth and the width will be of similar proportions.

Layout Paper

Initial sketches can be made on any type of paper – one of the cheapest to use, incidentally, is decorator's lining paper.

Once your ideas start to firm up, use **layout** grade drawing paper. This can be found in most art supplies shops. It is thin, so, by overlaying sheets and re-drawing, you can build up a succession of images. The project drawings in this book can be enlarged with a photocopier, then, if you wish, changes could be made using layout paper.

Draw with Felt-Tipped Pens

Only simple line drawings, rather than highly detailed sketches, are necessary, so you do not have to be a great artist. You do, however, need to produce a design capable of being carved with the tools you have, so give some thought to their widths when drawing. It helps to draw with bold lines, and to avoid tiny areas of detail. Felt-tipped pens, broad soft pencils, or charcoal sticks are all equally good. Transfer sketches to the wood using carbon paper – the blue pencil grade, or the erasable, graphite-coated type.

Five-Point Plan (Figs 27–30)

Step 1 **(Fig 27)** Using layout paper, start by marking out the size of the wood.

Step 2 **(Fig 28)** Draw a centre line.

Step 3 **(Fig 29)** You may need to draw only one half of the design. Include location points to align the drawing on the wood when the paper is reversed.

Step 4 For three-dimensional work also draw side and rear views, working to the size of the wood. Include centre line and locating points.

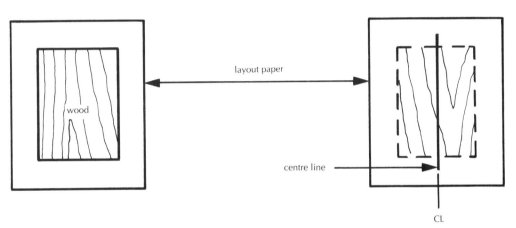

Fig 27   Using layout paper, mark wood size . . .

Fig 28   . . . mark in the centre line . . .

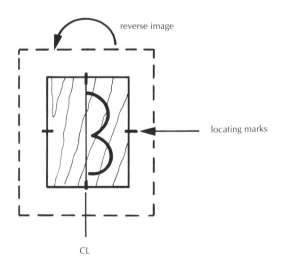

Fig 29   . . . then mark location points, and only draw one half of the design if it is to be reversed.

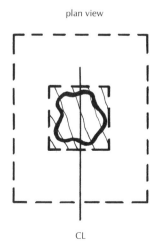

Fig 30   Make a plan view, showing size of wood and centre lines.

Step 5 (Fig 30) Make a plan view (of the subject seen from above), using all or half of the form, depending on whether or not it is matched. Start with size of wood. Use a centre line.

How to Transfer the Drawing to the Wood

Step 1 (Fig 31) Mark the block with **centre lines** on each side, on the top and on the bottom. If the drawing is to be reversed, then mark an additional horizontal line at the mid-point.

Step 2 (Figs 32–34) Start with the front view.
- Trim the paper to the size of the wood.
- Cut V-shaped nicks into the paper at either end of the centre line, and of the horizontal line, if one has been used.
- Using masking tape, fix the drawing to the front side of the block, lining up the vertical V-cuts with the centre line drawn on the wood. If only one half of the design is drawn, align the mid-point V-cut with the horizontal line as well.

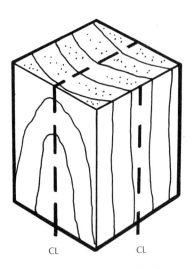

Fig 31 *Mark up the carving block with centre lines on each face.*

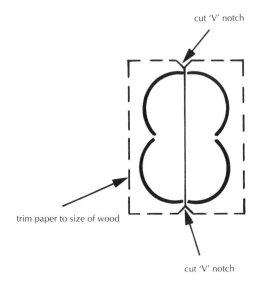

Fig 32 *Trim paper to size of wood. Then cut 'V' notches at centre line ends.*

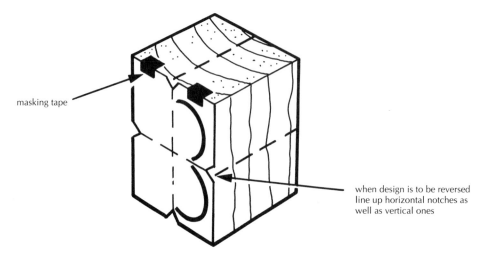

Fig 33 *Fix the drawing to the wood using masking tape. Use 'V' notches to line up the centre lines.*

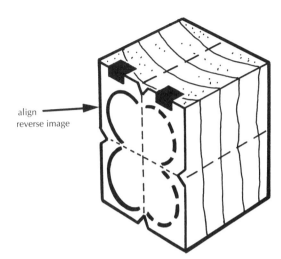

align
reverse image

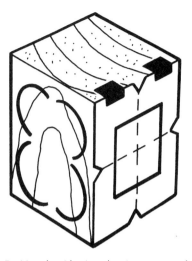

Fig 34   After the first imprint, align the reverse image.

Fig 35   Position the side view drawing – reverse for the other side.

• To copy the drawing onto the wood use either pencil grade (blue), or erasable graphite carbon paper. Copy with a ballpoint pen for a sharp outline and use different coloured ink to go over the original, to avoid missing any parts of the design.

• If necessary, reverse the drawing to give the second half of the design and to locate the V-cuts, then complete the carbon imprint.

Step 3 (Fig 35) Side-view drawings need to be positioned using V-cuts, which can be matched to vertical and horizontal lines on the wood; then carbon copy them onto the wood. Plan views are marked out in the same way.

Safety

Woodcarving is a relatively safe pastime, always providing sensible precautions are taken.

Naturally, if you pick up a carving tool by its cutting edge, sooner or later you are going to cut yourself. But it is unlikely you would intentionally do this; most people would pick up a tool by its handle. It is when you are in a hurry, or working on a cluttered bench that accidents happen. So try and keep the number of tools out on the bench down to only a few. When there is a need for more tools to be out at one time, get into the habit of laying them down with their handles pointing towards you.

The most common risk of cutting yourself is if you let the odd finger stray near to the blade tip. *Do not ever do it.*

Fig 37 shows how a gouge, or chisel for that matter, can be safely held when using hand pressure alone to carve. Note how the left hand (in right-

Fig 37   Correct way to hold a gouge when carving with hand pressure.

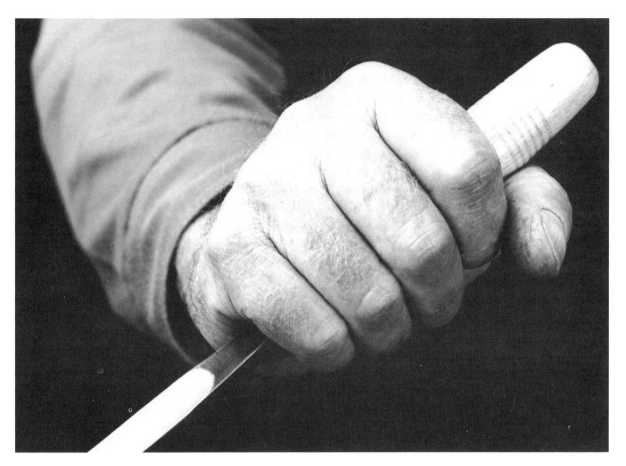

Fig 38   Correct way to hold a gouge when using a mallet.

handed use) is back from the tip, but at the same time, by resting the knuckles on the wood, a positive angle of cut, without wavering, is maintained. The knuckles also act as a pivot point when twisting cuts are made.

Fig 38 shows how the gouge should be held when a mallet is used. There are two points to note. Firstly the thumb is well out of the way. It will not be hit by the mallet. Secondly, the little finger is wrapped around the ferrule of the handle to prevent the gouge from slipping.

IMPORTANT SAFETY TIP

At all times cuts should be made **away from** your body, never towards it.

It should be obvious that the wood being carved must be secured to the bench, either directly or by using some form of workholder. Unfortunately, I have known instances when this has not been the case, usually when the carver has decided, on the spur of the moment, to make a small change while the work is just lying on the bench. That is when an accident will happen!

Apart from these specific points, everyday workshop safety practice should be clearly observed, including such things as the safe use of power tools, the wearing of safety glasses and the use of a dust mask, and the safe keeping of inflammable solvents.

Project One – Little Owl

There is no doubt that owls are always popular subjects for carving. Their upright shape is ideal for a first carving, since it is relatively uncomplicated. Also, we are probably more able to use our own interpretation of shape and form than with many other subjects, and this can be comforting to anyone just starting. If minor errors creep into the design, they will not matter too much, or they may not even be noticed at all. So let us start.

For a first-time carving it is best to keep things simple. Avoid difficult poses. Have the owl forward facing, rather than looking to one side. This project is based on a Scops Owl, found in mainland Europe. It is a small owl and is 'eared', which gives the face strong design lines.

CHOICE OF WOOD

Cherry is an ideal wood for this type of carving. Its bold grain goes well with the body shape. Allow for some wastage and choose a piece longer than needed. When trimmed at the ends, in case there are any hairline cracks, the minimum size needed for working is **9in×4in×4in (230mm×100mm×100mm)**. This will allow enough spare wood for screw fixing when mounting the base prior to carving.

Decide which way up it should be by feeling the lie of the grain. Run your fingers over the surface. It will feel smoother in one direction than the other. The **smooth lie** of the grain needs to run from **top** to **bottom**. Draw centre lines on each side, as well as on the top.

YOU WILL NEED	
³⁄₈in (10mm) No. 2	¹⁄₄in (6mm) No. 6
¹⁄₄in (6mm) No. 3	¹⁄₂in (13mm) No. 7
³⁄₄in (20mm) No. 4	¹⁄₄in (6mm) No. 9
³⁄₄in (20mm) No. 5	¹⁄₈in (3mm) No. 11
¹⁄₄in (6mm) No. 41 V-tool	

DRAWINGS (Figs 39–42)

- Fig 39 shows half the front view. It will be reversed to give a matching left-hand shape, as described in Chapter 4.
- Fig 40 shows the side view. Note the line marked *Visual Axis*. This gives the owl its forward tilt.
- Fig 41 is the approximate plan view. Use this only as a guide to the final sectional shape.
- Fig 42 is the rear view of the body and is a guide to both tail shape and wing position.

Dimensions

Whilst the actual overall height of the carving is only 8in (200mm), start with a longer piece of timber. As previously mentioned, this will permit the base to be trimmed back to remove screw holes left when the wood was held for carving.

Proportions

The height of the head is 2in (50mm) and the body 4in (100mm), giving a total height above the base of 6in (150mm). Note that the feet and tail are formed from wood being part of the base. A ratio of two-thirds the height for both the width and the depth has been used. Thus, each measures 4in (100mm).

Allowing for the extra length for the screw holes in the bottom of the block the working dimensions are **9in×4in×4in (230mm×100mm×100mm)**.

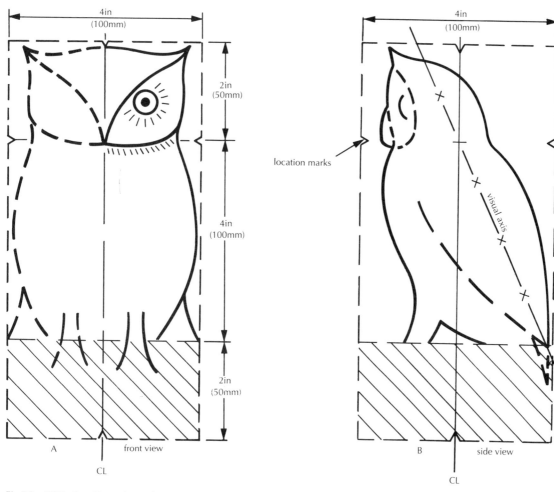

Fig 39   'A' Project One – front view.

Fig 40   'B' Project One – side view (profile).

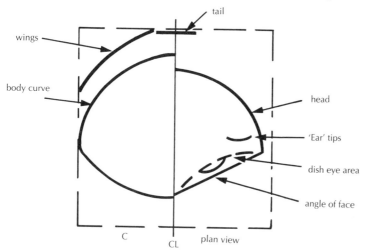

Fig 41   'C' Project One – plan view.

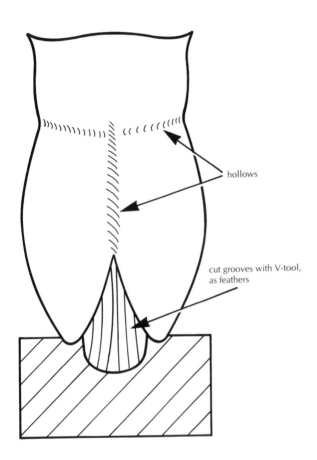

Fig 42   'D' Project One – rear view.

hollows

cut grooves with V-tool, as feathers

Fig 43   Project One. Front drawing taped on block. (Note location cuts on paper.)

Imprinting the Front View (Fig 43)

Enlarge the working drawings or, if you prefer, make your own using layout paper. Follow the method of transferring the drawings to the wood, covered in Chapter 4.

Note the front-view drawing has locating marks where the head and body join. Once the first half imprint has been made it is a good idea to strike a line from this location point around each side of the wood. This will assist lining up the other half of the front drawing, and will make sure the head is equally placed.

Imprinting the Side Views (Figs 44 and 45)

If the wood is to be cut with a bandsaw, only one side view is needed. If hand-sawing is to be carried

out, put a reverse drawing onto the other side of the wood, taking care it lines up correctly. Then, as the saw is used, the depth of cut can be checked. Mark waste areas with hatched lines.

If the imprint is in any way unclear, overdraw with a felt-tipped pen.

V-Tool the Outline (Fig 46)

To prevent accidentally sawing into the design, it is a wise precaution to cut a trench around the outline of the drawing, just in the waste wood, with the No. 41 V-tool. This acts as a safety net. Saw cuts leave distressed wood, and the safety net should prevent them from marking the actual carving.

Fig 44 *Drawing imprinted onto wood.*

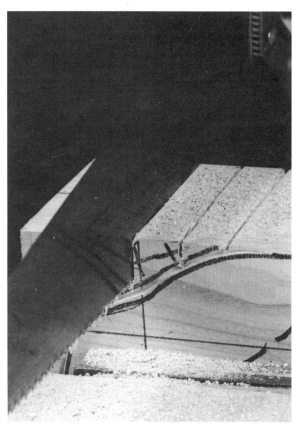

Fig 45 *Sawing waste wood by hand.*

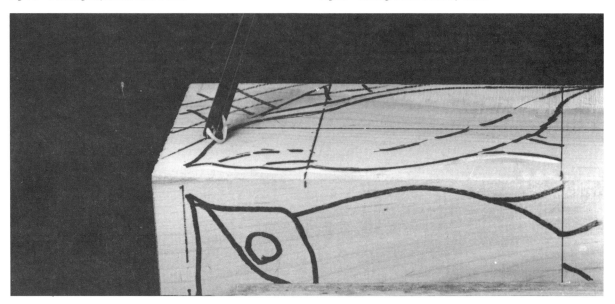

Fig 46 *V-tool cutting outline.*

Fig 47   Sawn stop-cuts enable waste to be chopped out.

REMOVING THE WASTE WOOD BY HAND (Fig 47)

Easily accessed waste areas present little problem. They are simply removed with straight saw cuts. Curved parts of the design, however, have to be gouged out. First make a series of saw cuts across the wood at close intervals. Keep the saw level, so that the depth of cut is even. It helps to have the drawing on both sides of the wood. These cuts make it easier to chop the wood out in little blocks without fear of the gouge becoming stuck. They also stop the wood splitting ahead of the cut. The process is carried out until all the surplus wood has been removed. Use a gouge with a steep sweep, like the No. 7, or No. 9.

BANDSAWING THE WASTE (Fig 48)

Preparing the wood with a bandsaw is a far quicker process. Use a narrow contour blade, which will cope better with tight curves.

One real advantage of using a bandsaw is that the shape of the blank can be cut from two directions; from the front and from the side. Cut the front view first. Then put back the waste and hold in place with masking tape while the side-view cut is made.

RE-MARK FEATURES (Fig 49)

Immediately after cutting, re-draw any missing features and cut round with the V-tool.

Workholding

Up to this point the wood can be held in an ordinary

Fig 48   When bandsawing, front waste can be temporarily held in place with masking tape whilst the profile is cut.

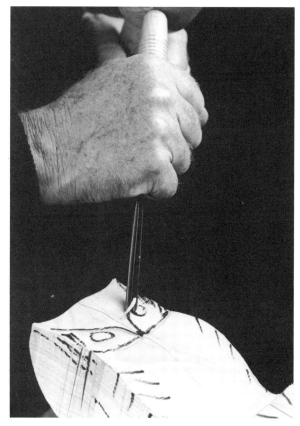

Fig 49   V-tool features.

bench-vice. If this type of vice is going to be used all the way through, use the mounting method described in Chapter 1. Otherwise, now is the time to fix the wood to the workholder faceplate, using pre-drilled screw holes.

ROUGH-SHAPING THE WOOD (Figs 50 and 51)

This stage, technically called **bosting in** is when all the rough shaping takes place. When it is complete, no flat areas should remain, other than those required by the design. Correctly done, the process of roughing out (bosting in and roughing out are the same thing) transforms the squareness of the original block into inter-linking curved surfaces.

Step 1   (Fig 50)   Start with short strokes to remove the edges of the block. Note how the cuts are being made back into the wood. Cutting the other way would result in the wood splitting, as there would not be any supporting timber for the last part of the cut. Work diagonally when cutting with the run of the grain.

Step 2   (Fig 51)   Once the initial cuts have been made, lengthen the strokes. Look for longer shavings.

To round the shape, raise the handle slightly as the cut is made. This adjusts the angle of the bevel, keeping the cutting edge in contact with the wood all the time.

Generally, it is best not to cut in the direction of the grain. Cut across it (as shown in Fig 51), or diagonally.

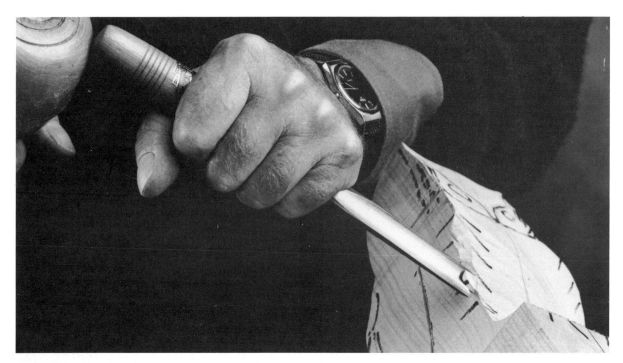

Fig 50 Work the sides first.

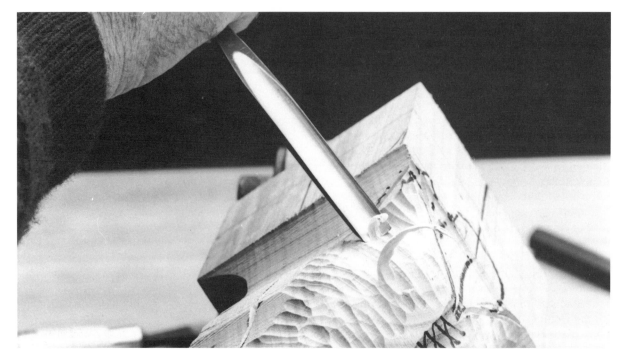

Fig 51 Keep adjusting the cutting angle for long cuts.

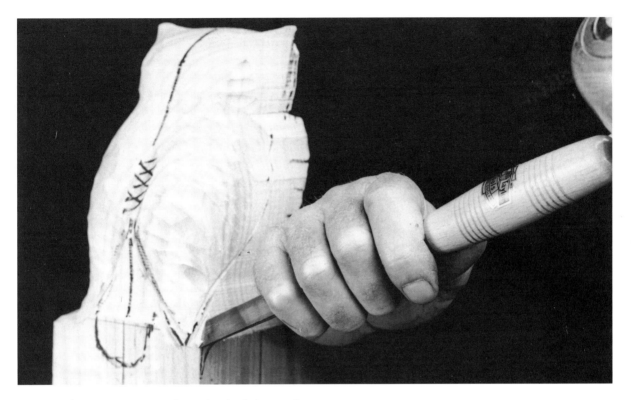

Fig 52   Stab-cutting in waste avoids stressing the design wood.

Use a quick-cut gouge, such as the ½in (13mm) No. 7 to remove wood speedily. Also, it helps when cutting hollows, as the corners of the blade are less likely to catch in the surface.

Whilst shaping is taking place it is vital to keep re-drawing the centre line as it is cut away. The reason is that the density of the wood varies, depending on how close it originally was to the tree centre. When the density is lower you tend to take deeper cuts and remove more wood. This will throw the carving out of balance, although you may not notice it is happening until it is too late. Centre lines help to prevent this, as they provide a visual reference.

needs to be removed so that these parts can be exposed. Do not overdo this, though, or the owl will appear to stand on tiptoe. Use the ¾in (20mm) No. 5 gouge, then you will avoid taking too much wood off with each cut.

Periodically, use your fingers to check the shape of the body for humps and bumps. Often you can better feel where there is excess wood, rather than see it.

While the shape is being developed, be prepared to make design changes. For example, if you uncover some attractively marked wood that was not previously visible, 'go with the wood'; do not stick rigidly to the design.

DEVELOPING THE SHAPE (Fig 52)

Up to now the work of boasting in has concentrated on the wood originally sawn roughly to shape. Some parts of the design, like the tail and the wing tips for example, are, at this stage of their development, integral with the base. Wood from the sides of the base

SHAPING THE BACK (Fig 53)

It is useful to position the carving so that you can see one half of the back, while you work the other half, as this will help you to get a better match to the shape. The way the wood is held in this picture, all of the back can be seen.

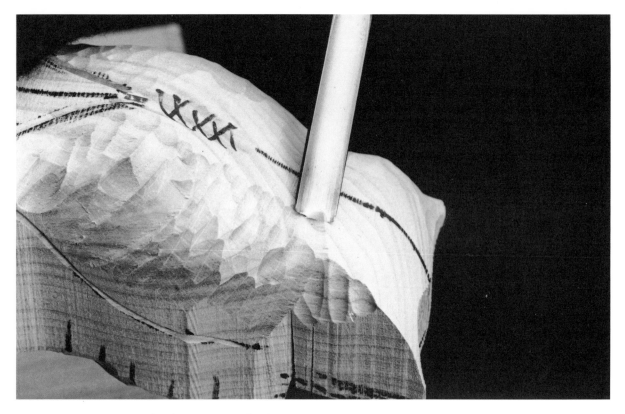

Fig 53   Use a steeper sweep than the curve to avoid tool snagging.

At the junction of the top of the wings and the lower part of the head, there is a definite change of contour. This is where the gouge is shown, and it marks the curve of the shoulders back to the base of the head. (Note there is no neck in the true sense.) The ½in (13mm) No. 7 should be used.

THE WINGS (Fig 54)

The wings envelop the body; thus, the widest part of the carving, viewed from the front, covers the leading edges of each wing. These edges need to be defined, so that the body appears to curve under them. Cut with the ¼in (6mm) No. 9, to give a rounded bottom to the line of the wing, which will then have a 'softer' look than if cut with the V-tool. Make the cut on a shallow angle to the run of the grain, for a smoother look.

FORMING THE LEGS

To make the legs stand forward of the body, hollow between them, in the middle, and on either side. Do not cut too deeply or you may have problems cleaning out the waste, unless you have a spoon-shaped gouge.

As this is a stylized owl, the feet need only be suggestively formed and not cut in any detail. It is easier if only two talons are shown. Draw them onto the wood, then cut around them with the ⅛in (3mm) No. 11 to give a rounded outline. Shape the top surface of each talon with the No. 2 skew chisel, and finally, sand them.

SHAPING THE HEAD (Figs 55–57)

The owl's face angles back on either side of the beak, to allow side vision. Whilst in real life the angle is quite acute, you may find this detracts from the look

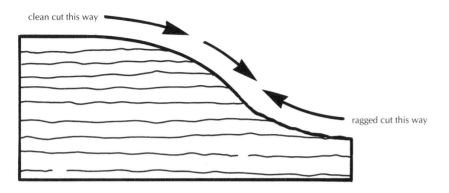

clean cut this way

ragged cut this way

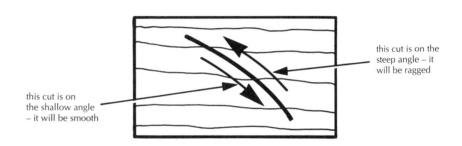

this cut is on the steep angle – it will be ragged

this cut is on the shallow angle – it will be smooth

Fig 54 Downhill, not uphill for clean cuts. Cut on the shallow angle of the grain.

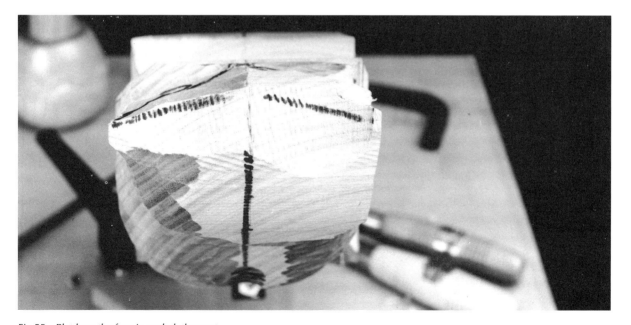

Fig 55 Plot how the face is angled, then cut.

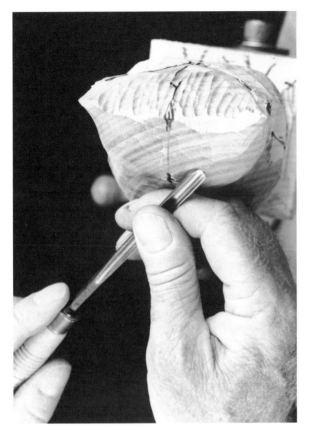

Fig 56   Work the 'ears' back to midway on the head.

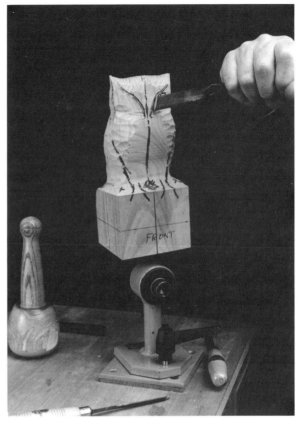

Fig 57   Stab-cut the shape – work in the waste.

of the carving. I prefer to work the face using only a fairly shallow angle for the side vision.

At the same time the brow can be rounded, both from side to side as well as from top to bottom. As this is done, the 'ears' move back to almost the mid-point depth of the head.

Cut the shape of the beak, and the shape of the brow over the eyes up to the 'ears', with the ¾in (20mm) No. 4. Work the left and right sides progressively to maintain their symmetry.

Still using the No. 4 gouge, define where the face meets the body. With the carving held horizontally, or upright if you prefer, stab-cut along the lower line of the face, then trim the body to curve inwards below the face. Leave the face plain for the moment.

SMOOTHING THE SURFACE (Figs 58 and 59)

Use the ¾in (20mm) No. 4 gouge to 'plane' the large surface areas, to remove the cuts made during the roughing out process. This is preferable to rasping the wood, which often leaves score marks. In order not to dig in too deeply, keep the gouge bevel rubbing the wood all the time. Just raise the handle a fraction to make paring cuts. With practice it is possible to achieve a very clean surface. If you find it difficult to use the gouge like this, then there will be no choice but to use a wood rasp.

Some parts will defy gouge smoothing, whether this is on account of their shape, or because the grain prevents clean cutting. In this case, small riffler files, or coarse sanding paper, will be needed.

At this stage you will be able to work over the whole of the carving by cutting, rasping or sanding.

Fig 58   See the difference between clean gouge cuts, and rasp distress marks.

Fig 59   A riffler file will trim 'tight' places.

THE EYES (Fig 60)

Note that one of the main features of the design is the saucer shapes surrounding the eyes. Form these first, using the ½in (13mm) No. 7, followed by smoothing cuts with the ¾in (20mm) No. 5.

Eyes can be simple slits, cut with the V-tool. They can be fully open, or half closed. If you choose either of these they will need to be modelled. Do not be put off by the prospect of this, as it is not difficult to shape eyes.

The eyes should be set halfway between the top and bottom of the head. Use parallel lines crossing the centre line at right angles to ensure they are level.

Mark the eye outline. Stab-cut this with a suitably shaped gouge. In this project the ¼in (6mm) No. 6 longpod was used. It is best to test all of the cuts on scrapwood before using them on the work.

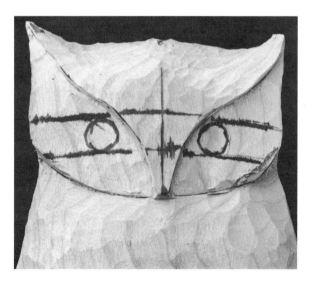

Fig 60   Location lines must cross the centre line at right angles.

Bisect the eyeball with a horizontal line. Then use the ¹/₄in (6mm) No. 3 gouge, inverted, so that the inside of the blade forms the basis of the eyeball. Increase the curve of the eyeball to the horizontal line using the No. 2 skew chisel.

A nail with the point rounded can be used to simulate the pupil. If necessary, it can be enlarged by lightly rotating the small No. 9 gouge.

SHAPE OF PLINTH

Give some thought to the shape of the plinth you are going to use, since it is a vital part of any sculpture. As shown, a rectilinear shape of plinth was chosen to contrast with the owl. There are times when the plinth could be integral, or complementary to the subject, as the branch of a tree would be.

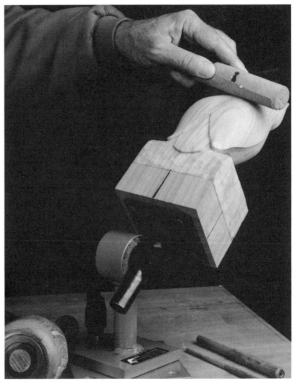

Fig 62   Sanding sticks.

TYPE OF FINISH (Figs 61 and 62)

Decide which type of finish you prefer – smooth or textured. In this picture you will see I have texture cut one half of the front of the body, leaving the rest smooth, to give you a guide as to the effect tooling the surface creates. Use the ¹/₄in (6mm) No. 6 gouge. Make small cuts, which can be spaced and arranged to simulate feathers.

It is possible to combine both treatments. For example, the face and the wings can be left smooth, whilst the remainder is tooled.

Whichever finish you choose, it will be necessary to prepare the surface of the wood by sanding. Full details of finishing techniques are covered in Chapter 11, but briefly, the preparation should ensure that a blemish-free surface is obtained. It is a good idea to use abrasive paper wrapped around a piece of dowel rod cushioned with leather.

The bare wood needs to be sealed prior to waxing. There are various ways this can be done and they are fully covered in the chapter on finishing techniques.

Fig 61   Smooth or textured, which do you prefer?

Fig 63   Finished carving of the owl.

7

Project Two – The Cottager's Pig

━━━━━━━ YOU WILL NEED ━━━━━━━

Wood: Elm
Size: Length 9in (230mm); width 5½in (140mm);
  height 5in (127mm).
Carving Tools:

¼in (6mm) No. 3	¼in (6mm) No. 6
¾in (20mm) No. 4	½in (13mm) No. 7
¾in (20mm) No. 5	¼in (6mm) No. 9
¼in (6mm) No. 41 V-tool	

Classic pig breeds, like the Gloucester Old Spot, and the Wessex Saddleback, make ideal subjects for learning about three-dimensional form in the horizontal pose. Think in terms of a real porker lying dozing after being well fed. To carve it successfully, you will need to be aware of the fundamental aspects of three-dimensional thinking, namely, which parts stick out beyond the basic shape. These will include the ears, the muscles of the forelegs and the hind legs, the bulge of the belly, and of course the tail. Within reason, the more emphasis you give to these the better. Knowing that they exist is not enough. You need to 'see' them in your mind's eye, for they all are important stages along the three-dimensional learning curve.

CHOOSING THE WOOD

Clearly, a recumbent fat sow will have a spread of width greater than that usually associated with animals when they are lying down. So, the very first thing is to try and visualize the bulging shape. When you are able to see what the shape will involve, it is easier to judge the size of wood needed.

Once the image is fixed in your mind, it will be obvious that you are going to need a piece of timber that is wider than it is thick. This will provide sufficient material for shaping the belly, the muscles and the ears.

Think how the tail is likely to be shaped. Most people would expect a pig to have a curly tail. You will need to take this into account when planning the overall length.

Pigs are seldom glossy. They love to be grubbing about in mud, and at best are described as 'rough' creatures. This should give a clue to type of wood to be used. With a bland, close-grained timber, like Lime or Sycamore, the surface could seem too plain and sleek if finished smooth. It could be texture cut, but the light colour would not be very appropriate. Woods like Elm, Chestnut, or Oak, with their coarser grain and browner look would be better. I carved the project in Elm that had been subjected to a slight wet rot. This caused dark streaks in the wood, compatible, I thought, with the pig concept.

Another reason for choosing wood of one of these species is that it is more likely to be available in large pieces, sufficient for the height and width needed for this project. The block of Elm I used was enough for the pig to be 8¾in (220mm) long with a body height of 4¾in (120mm) and width of 5½in (140mm).

DRAWINGS (Figs 64–66)

The drawings are constructed in the same manner as in Project 1. For this carving, the plan view is vital, as it allows you to ascertain the width of wood needed for the muscles and the ears. A sectional drawing is also useful. It will help to establish body contours and tail shape.

It is essential there should be no flat parts to the body; it should all be made up of gentle curves. To achieve this the body size needs to be drawn less than the full size of the wood. This will permit all the curves to be sawn without hindrance. If the drawing is 'tight', with little or no surplus wood surrounding it, flat spots are sure to occur. These can prove difficult to eradicate completely later on.

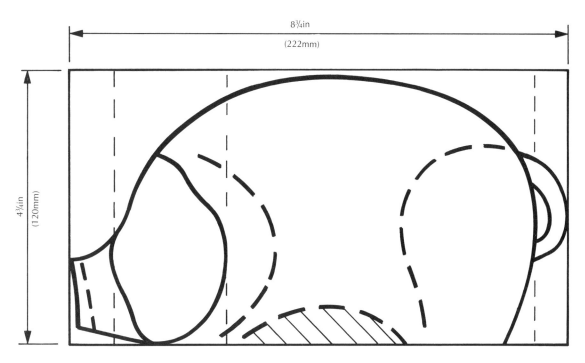

Fig 64   Project Two – profile view.

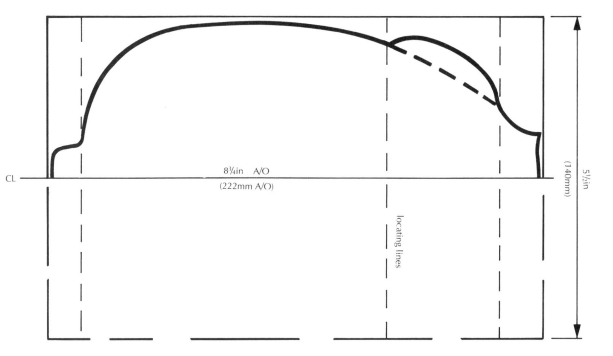

Fig 65   Project Two – one half plan view.

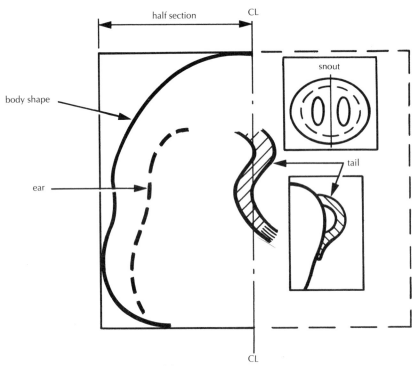

Fig 66   Project Two – sectional shapes and data.

Transfer the Drawings onto the Wood

Use the same method of transfer that you used in Project One, and mark up the wood with both the plan and the profile views. Location lines will be required for positioning the ears. Note that the leading edges of the ears should be set well forward to cover the eyes. At this stage it does no harm at all to make the ears oversize. They represent a dominant feature of the carving, the impact of which could become lost should they finish up too small.

Card templates of both plan and profile views can be useful, both to aid initial shaping and to keep as reference if you think you will be going on to make more pigs in the future.

OUTLINE SAWING

Because of its symmetrical shape, either of the two basic methods of sawing the waste, by hand or with a bandsaw, can be used. Remember, it pays to outline the drawings with a V-tool, to create a safety net.

A MORE ADVANCED TECHNIQUE

Although I would not recommend this third method if this is only your second carving, since it relies on a lot of visualization, you may wish to try it in the future. Briefly, it consists of taking the squared block and shaping it with gouges until it looks like a loaf of home-baked bread. Then the design is drawn onto the wood by hand and shaping continues with the minimum amount of sawing. The advantage of this method is that an asymmetrical shape can be produced, which it may be impossible to cut in the conventional way.

After sawing, mount the wood either directly to a workholder, or to a wood block for holding in a bench vice. Keep some of the sawdust for use later.

ROUGHING OUT THE SHAPE

Mark the outline shape of the ears with shallow V-tool cuts to start with, to allow any subsequent change to their shape to be made. Then draw in the parts needed for the belly, and the fore and hind quarters.

Mark a centre line along the length of the body to help you detect any drift of shape caused by varying density when the wood is shaped. Cross the centre line at right-angles to fix points of the design, like leg muscles. Always replace the line when it gets cut away.

SHAPING THE BODY (Figs 67–69)

There can be considerable amounts of wood to remove before you obtain any roundness of the body. This process can be speeded up by making some saw cuts along the upper edges of the body. Start by cutting a notch just behind the ears, then make a series

of cuts along the top of the body. Chop out the small blocks formed by the saw cuts using the No. 5 gouge.

After this, remove excess wood to produce the roundness of the body by cutting with the 1/2in (13mm) No. 7 gouge. Along the sides of the body, where less wood needs to be removed, use the flatter gouges like the No. 4 and No. 5. Make only very shallow cuts. If you make deep cuts you may remove more wood than is necessary. This could cause problems. Again, re-mark parts of the design as they get cut away.

ROLL THE BOTTOM EDGE (Fig 70)

The bottom edge of the pig needs to be rolled over. This will produce a shadow line, when the carving is placed on a shelf or table, which helps to give it less of a static look. The rolling shape can be cut with the No. 4 gouge. Use it inverted so that the inner curve

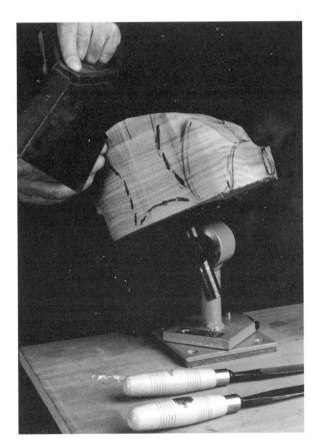

Fig 67 Saw cuts on edges help waste removal . . .

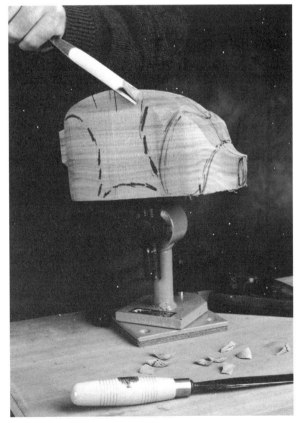

Fig 68 . . . waste can then be easily chopped out.

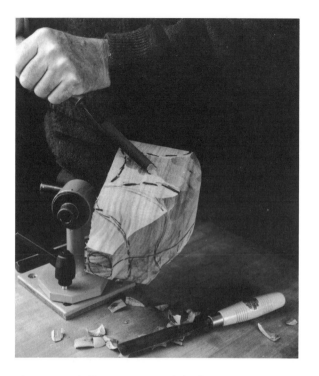

Fig 69 Use shallow cuts on extended sides.

of the blade forms the shape. Repeat this cut as body shaping progresses.

FORMING THE EARS (Fig 71)

There is an old saying about not being able to make a silk purse out of a sow's ear – perhaps it is true. But one thing is certain. The ears are one of the main features of this carving, and much of its success will depend on how they are formed by shape and contour. They provide the chance to give the pig a sense of being alive. This can be done by flipping up one edge, as if the ear were twitching. Small design touches like this can transform the work and it will cease to remain simply a piece of decorated wood. Use your own ideas of interpretation. Align the tops of the ears by using parallel lines crossing the centre line.

Using the No. 4 and No. 5 gouges, stab-cut the rear edge of each ear to the required shape. Note that in the picture the gouge is being held upright. This is to give a vertical cut, with the bevel facing *outwards* to make a convex shape. When the cut needs to

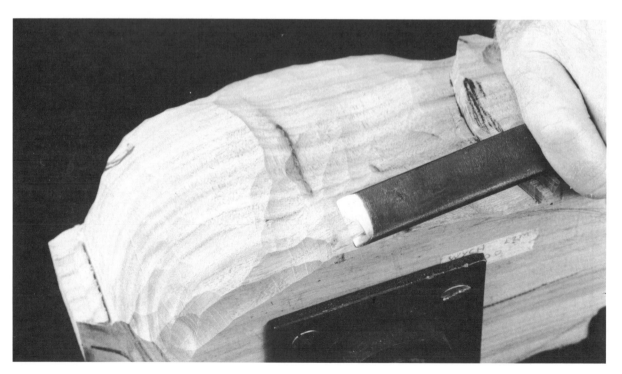

Fig 70 Shape using the inside curve of the gouge.

Fig 71   Stab-cut to the outline.

curve inwards for a concave shape, the bevel is placed *towards* the design. Then the gouge has to lean *away* from the design, to allow the bevel to make a perpendicular cut. If this seems complex just try it out by holding the gouge close to the shapes you have drawn for the ears. The method should then become clear.

Repeat the stab-cutting process to shape the front edges, making sure the ears cover much of the face. Avoid cutting too deep, or the marks will still show when the carving is finished.

NAPE OF NECK (Fig 72)

To make the ears stand out, the width of the adjacent parts, like the nape of the neck and the tops of the shoulders, has to be reduced. This is fundamental to three-dimensional carving. To make one element of the design stand out, surrounding levels have to be taken back. In this case they are the nape of the neck and the spread of the shoulders. Later you will also need to establish the final width of the head.

Fig 72   Reduce the wood at the nape of the neck.

FORELEGS (Fig 73)

Once the shoulders and nape have been fixed, it then remains to set the upper and lower parts of the forelegs at their correctly inclined angles. If you have difficulty in visualizing these angles, try the following experiment:

• Sit on a low chair or stool, sideways on to a mirror, so that you can see the reflection of your shoulder as well as your arm and thigh. Place the palms of your hands on your thighs and hunch up your shoulders, bringing them forward a little. See how the shoulder takes on a rounded shape. Use this type of shape when you position the pig's shoulders.

• Keeping the hunched position, check where your elbows are. Note how the arm angles out somewhat from the shoulder to the elbow, and how it then slants back inwards to allow the hand to rest on the thigh. The forelegs of the pig have a similar shape. They angle out from the shoulder to produce the

muscle area, until the leg joint is reached, and then return inwards to lie under the ears. Once you are able to visualize what happens, you should have little difficulty when it comes to carving them.

CARVING THE HEAD (Fig 74)

Before any wood is removed, try one other exercise in three-dimensional thinking. Imagine for a moment what shape of head you would see if you could lift the ears off. Then try and hold the shape in your mind. The reason for this is that, as you carve, you must construct the curves which relate to the shape of the head itself and for a moment ignore the ears. By doing this, the shape of the brow, for example, will look as if it continues on underneath the ears. If you do not do this, the head and ears may look as if they blend together.

The brow and face are both endgrain areas. They

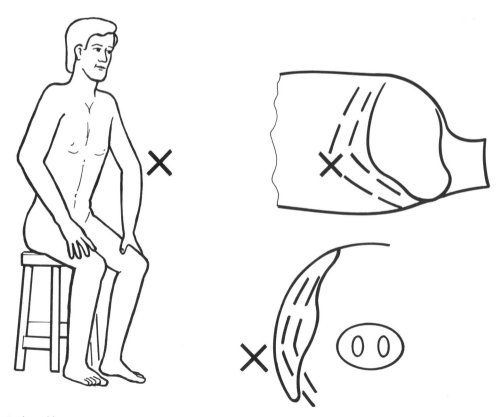

Fig 73   Body and legs.

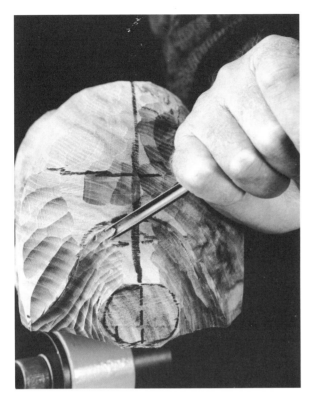

Fig 74   Use the small No. 9 gouge for cutting endgrain.

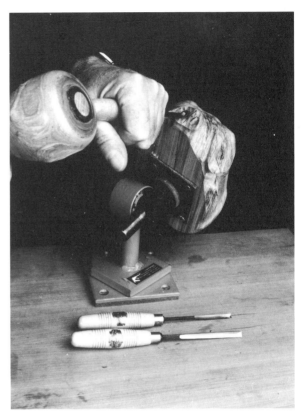

Fig 75   Form the nostrils with the ¼in (6mm) No. 9.

are best cut initially using the ¼in (6mm) No. 9 gouge, as its narrow edge will cause less distress to the wood. Remember, the wider the cut, the greater the risk of cell-ends fracturing and causing the surface to become pitted. Once the bulk of the waste has been removed, the surface can be smoothed using a gouge with a flatter sweep, like the No. 3.

The brow is shaped just like the human forehead, curving from side to side as well as up to the crown which, in the case of the pig, is the mid-point between the ears.

THE SNOUT (Fig 75)

Notice how, in Fig 75, the snout is shown as a flat-tened circle. The shape can be made with the ¾in (20mm) No. 5 gouge. The same tool can be used to dish the front of the snout on either side of the centre line, or, if you prefer the dish-like shapes to be deeper, use the ½in (13mm) No. 7. Cut the nostrils with the ¼in (6mm) No. 9.

THE REAR END AND TAIL (Fig 76)

When working on this portion of the pig, remember much of the wood will be endgrain. Like the head it will need cutting with razor-sharp tools, preferably of narrow width.

Make sure the rear is shaped equally on either side of the tail, and that it has the right contours.

Fig 76 shows the tail S-shaped. It is essential this is drawn on the wood with a *centre line*, and also that the tail locates at the centre line of the body. Nothing looks worse than a tail carved off-centre! As you shape the tail, keep replacing its own centre line.

Once the shape of the tail has been drawn onto the wood, mark it in with the V-tool. Then cut the surplus wood away on either side using the ¼in (6mm) No. 9. As the remaining waste wood lessens, start to incise the shape with stab cuts, using the ¾in (20mm) No. 4 or No. 5 for the wider curves, and the small No. 6 and No. 3 for the steeper bends. Trim to size

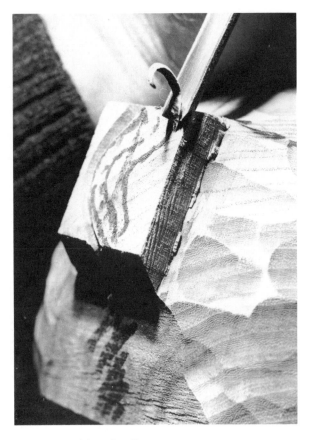

Fig 76   V-tool the tail outline.

and then roll the upper edges over to form the rounded shape of the main part of the tail. Incidentally, a pig's tail is like a piece of string with a tassel at one end. Later, when the wood has been smoothed, the tassel-like hairs can be formed with light V-tool cuts.

While it is not necessary to pierce through to produce the 'cup-hook', if the wood shows no tendency to be brittle you may want to do so. Do not worry too much about the tail breaking off. If it does, you can just shorten the body and carve a new one! Drill a tiny pilot hole, then widen to shape with the $\frac{1}{8}$in (3mm) No. 11, taking care not to snap the tip of the tool. Use a small file, or a slim strip of sanding paper, to shape the hole further.

You may wish to opt for the safer alternative, as I did, and angle-cut on either side of the tail to create shadow-producing recesses. I used the $\frac{1}{4}$in (6mm) No. 6 longpod to cut the curve of the recess, and the small No. 3 to take off the waste along the rear of the body.

FINISH (Fig 77)

As explained in Project One, there are various methods of finishing a carving. These are explained in the chapter on finishing techniques (Chapter 11). At this stage a couple of points are worth noting.

• If rasping has been carried out there are bound to be scratch marks. In the normal course of events these would be removed during the sanding stage. But you may find some of the grain has lifted, or torn out completely, because the rasp has been worked against the lie of the grain. Believe me, it is very easy for this to happen, especially if a coarse-toothed rasp has been used. These marks are virtually impossible to eradicate by sanding. It is far better to cut them out and re-shape the surrounding wood.

• At the start of this project I suggested you kept some of the sawdust. Now is the time to use it to fill in the holes in the base left by the mounting screws. Mix the sawdust with some resin wood adhesive so it becomes like plastic wood, and use it as a filler.

Fig 77   Project Two carving completed.

8

Project Three
Waves with Leaping Dolphin

This project and the two that follow it have been designed to help you to learn how to incorporate 'movement' into your work.

DESIGN CONCEPT

Generally speaking, the more there is a sense of movement, the less likely the carving will look 'wooden', or remain just a decorated piece of timber. The feeling of movement is best created by using construction lines which flow and curve sympathetically with the grain, or figuring, of the wood. There is more chance of this being successful if the design is such that the eye is permitted to start viewing the subject at the base line and is then carried up and away, following the shape of the carving. This may mean having to modify an anatomical detail here or there, but this does not matter. The essential thing is to achieve the sense of movement. For example, in this project the dolphin is powering itself out of the water. Showing something of the tail tends to emphasize the move-

ment, even if it is only suggested. Similarly, the way the waves are linked to the body, and rise up around it, help to create the impression that something powerful is going on.

PROFILE – THE DOMINANT VIEW (Fig 78)

In this carving, the profile is the dominant viewpoint. I started by sketching the side-on design before tackling the plan view. The weight of the dolphin is located towards the front, comprising the mass of the head and the forward part of the body. This can lead to instability, unless the base is made sufficiently long. For this reason, the length of the block was fixed initially at 9½in (240mm). This will allow for some possible shortening once the true centre of gravity is known.

Fig 78 shows the profile used. Because the waves obscure part of the body, it is only necessary, first of all, to work on the dolphin's shape above the waterline; the remainder of the composition, comprising the waves and the tail in amongst them, can be finally fixed once the carving reaches the level of the water. It is obviously useful, though, to have some idea of what the body shape would be below water, and this data is drawn with a broken line.

CUTTING THE PROFILE

Apply the drawing with carbon paper, as previously described. Then, using the V-tool, cut, following the bold line, including the small blocks on either side of the body for the pectoral fins, cutting a little outside the drawn line of the shape.

Initial profile cutting up to the line of the waves gives maximum support whilst the upper part of the dolphin's body is being roughed out. This may tend

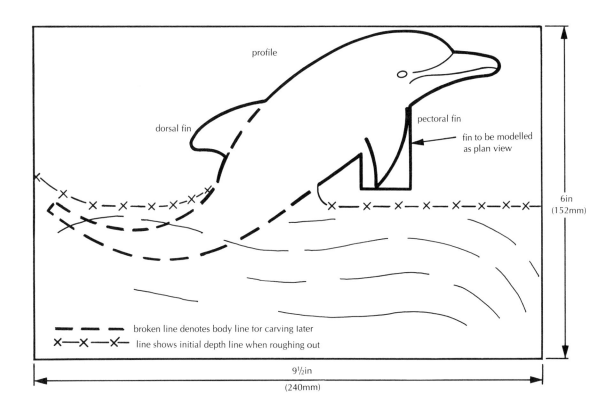

Fig 78   Project Three – profile view of the Dolphin.

to impede cutting the underside of the body some-what, but it is best to work in this manner. Apart from the added support, it does allow the carving to 'grow' out of the block with better flow of movement being likely, since minor adjustments can be made as you go along.

If a bandsaw is not being used, hand saw notches to form blocks for chopping out with a gouge, as described in the first project. Avoid allowing any saw cuts to penetrate below the waterline at this stage. Their marks could well be a nuisance later on when the waves are carved.

APPLYING THE PLAN VIEW (Fig 79)

Before this drawing can be copied onto the wood the top surface of the body will need to be flattened off by making shallow cuts with the ¾in (20mm) No. 3 gouge, or the ½in (13mm) fishtail version. The alternative is to rasp the wood, instead of using the gouges. Aim for a level surface, not one that is rounded over.

Draw the plan view free-hand, or use a card template. Follow only the bold outline, ending at the dorsal fin. There needs to be a centre line drawn down the length of the block. After marking out, cut round the plan view with the V-tool.

Fig 79   Project Three – plan views with fin/tail sections.

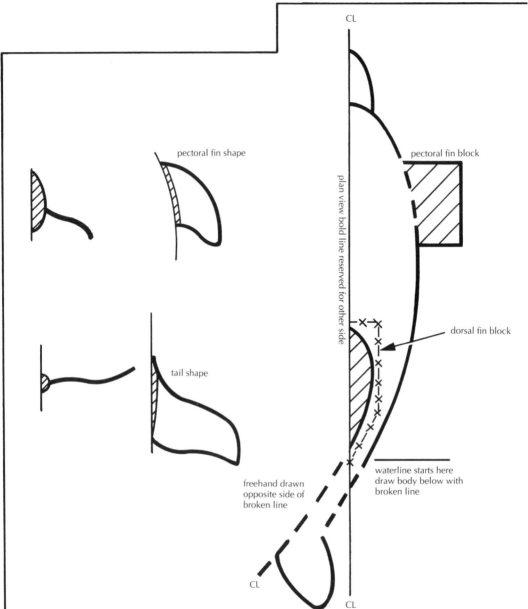

pectoral fin shape

CL

plan view bold line reserved for other side

pectoral fin block

dorsal fin block

tail shape

waterline starts here
draw body below with
broken line

freehand drawn
opposite side of
broken line

CL

CL

FORMING THE SIDES OF THE BODY

Reduce the sides of the body to a little more than the planned final width. As before, use a handsaw to cut notches and chop out the waste with the ¹/₂in (13mm) No. 7 gouge, still keeping the shape in block form. At this stage, it is really important that the sides remain as vertical as possible. Should they tend to incline outwards, the body will become fatter than planned. Once the bulk of the wood has been removed, trim to the final overall shape with the No. 3 and No. 4 gouges. When working on the sides of the body, you should angle the gouge so that the bevel cuts true and vertical.

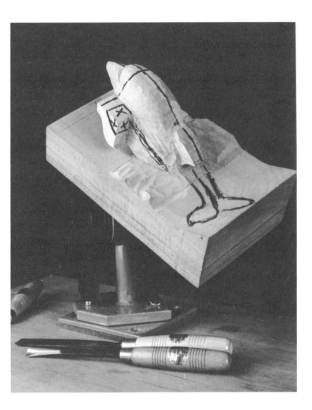

Fig 80 The fin block being roughed out.

PLOTTING THE FINS (Fig 80)

Once the body has been shaped in block form, plot the position of the pectoral fins. To match their location, use parallel lines, crossing the centre line at right angles. For the time being the fins can be left as two blocks, for shaping later. Allow some latitude by forming the blocks oversize. It should be possible to cut them to size with a small handsaw, but take care not to cut into the body area. If at all doubtful about your ability to cut accurately, angle the saw so that it cuts away from the drawn line.

Similarly, mark and form the block shape of the dorsal fin.

SHAPING THE BODY (Figs 81–84)

This is probably the most critical part of the carving.

Step 1 Decide how round the body needs to be. Fig 81 shows the sectional shapes used.

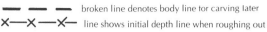

broken line denotes body line for carving later
line shows initial depth line when roughing out

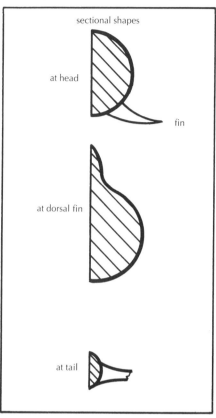

Fig 81 Project Three – sections of body shape.

Step 2 Remove any saw marks, or the distressed wood will continue to show when the dolphin is finished. Cut them out and pare back the surrounding wood.

TIP

When forming the sectional body shape, you have to be certain to maintain equal curves on either side. Remember that wood seldom has a consistent density. One side frequently proves easier to cut than the other, and this can lead to the shape becoming distorted. Do not just look at the work from the sides, in profile. You may not notice any imbalance occurring. Check from every angle. It is necessary to carry out as much of the shaping looking down from above, as from the front, or the sides.

Use centre lines on the sides of the body, as well as on the top and bottom surfaces, and replace them as soon as they are cut away.

Step 3 (Fig 82)   Mark in the approximate shape of the pectoral fins, viewed from the front, and draw in the underside of the body. This will give you some idea as to how much wood can be removed. Do not take too much wood away from the pectoral fins at this stage. When shaping the dorsal fin, bring the body and the fin together with a radius formed with the $\frac{1}{4}$in (6mm) No. 9. This will produce a soft and natural look. If cut with a shallow gouge, the junction will be too angular and harsh. Just let the two planes blend together.

Step 4 (Fig 83)   Continue to form the shape of the pectoral fins, by setting the angle of incline, and cutting out waste wood.

Step 5 (Fig 84)   Avoid making deep cuts when rounding the body. Use the shallower gouges as much as you can to form the convex shapes, such as

Fig 82   Mark the outline of the under belly and fin; front view.

Fig 83   Start shaping the fins.

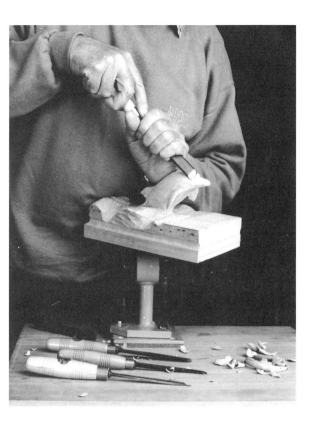

Fig 84   Round the head using the inverted No. 3 gouge.

the head and back. This may involve making shaping cuts with the gouge sweep inverted. Use the $^3/_4$in (20mm) No. 5 upside-down for the dome of the head. In concave areas, make conventional cuts with the $^1/_2$in (13mm) No. 7 or even the No. 9.

Use your sense of touch to detect any areas of excess wood.

SHAPING THE UNDER-BELLY

The fundamental point to note is that the belly has a flatter shape underneath, rather than being totally cylindrical. This flatness extends from the 'beak' to about halfway below the dorsal fin.

Once the body sides have been shaped, remove waste wood from under the belly. This will allow you to separate the pectoral fins from below. Try and carry out as much of this work as possible using gouges. Rasping will leave score marks which can be difficult to eradicate.

SHAPING THE FINS (Figs 85 and 86)

One of the most common errors is to place these fins in the wrong plane by lying them against the side of the body, instead of having them standing out away from it. If you look once more at Fig 78 and then at the plan view fin shape in Fig 79, the difference will be obvious. Incidentally, the reason for showing the fin as it is in the first drawing is to make certain a big enough block is left for shaping later on.

Step 1   (Fig 85)   Mark on the top side of the fin blocks the peripheral outline; mark on the ends the edge shape you would expect to see, and then check that your three-dimensional interpretation is correct before starting to cut.

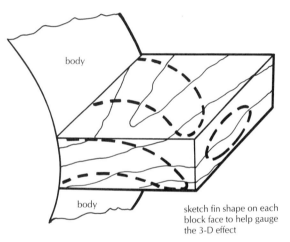

body

body

sketch fin shape on each block face to help gauge the 3-D effect

Fig 85   Think in 3-D – shape of pectoral fin.

Step 2   (Fig 86)   Because the fins will be standing out from the body, they will be, in the main, on short grain wood, and will therefore be weak. Fortunately, the fins are naturally quite fleshy, so keep them reasonably thick to retain strength, and feather the edges out as shown. You will need to treat them with care, and you will most probably wish to use a fine-cut rasp, or coarse sanding paper, for their final shaping. Work the dorsal fin in the same way.

Fig 86   Feather edge the fins – they will look less clumsy.

PREPARATION FOR A SMOOTH BODY FINISH

Carry out this stage before you commence carving the waves and tail. Whilst sanding and finishing techniques are covered separately, you may need to do some preparation at this stage to eradicate any deep or uneven tool cuts. Rasps can be used, but do keep in mind that the learning process will be better advanced by practising cutting with gouges. Use them as much as you can to prepare the wood for finishing. Tools like the shallow-cut gouges and the No. 6 longpod, as well as the No. 2 skew chisel, will work well. Just sometimes will it be safer to shape with a rasp, a riffler file, or even coarse abrasive paper.

Even at this stage, the carving can still start to go out of balance, so make certain that the centre line is replaced as soon as it is cut away. It is preferable to use a soft pencil, rather than a felt-tipped pen, so that the wood will not be indelibly stained.

FORMING THE TAIL AND THE WAVES (Figs 87–89)

Check the centre of gravity by moving the carving out over the bench edge until it starts to rock. Then decide if the base can be shortened at all.

Draw in the plan view of the tail and the remaining part of the body, if you have not done this already. To start with, both of these elements will be on a higher level than you will want them in the end. This is good, as this means that there will be ample wood in the remainder of the block for adjusting their angles to ensure continuity of body line. It will be necessary to judge both the tilt of the tail, and where it will finally lie. The reason for this is that the waves have to look as if they are washing against these parts of the dolphin.

Try to think of the tail, and the top of the body behind the dorsal fin, as being part of the same composition as the waves. This will mean having to model the waves progressively, as the tail and body

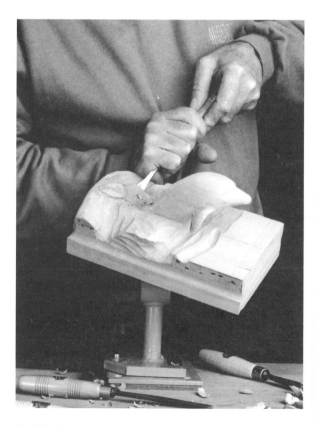

Fig 87   Making waves.

Fig 88   Have some waves splashing the body.

Fig 89 Bring a few waves over the sides.

are fashioned. Keep all the elements developing at the same rate of progress. If they are worked separately, with the tail and body being carved before the waves are worked, they will not look as good. Once the waves around the tail begin to assume their true shape, it will be possible to finalize the angle of the tail by tilting it, so that the trailing edge is higher than the front portion. At the same time, contours can be built in, to give a further feeling of movement.

The waves are integral with the base, and will need to be depicted on the sides as well as on the top. You could give all the base wave treatment if you wish, but if the lower parts of the sides are left plain more emphasis will be placed on the carved portion.

Draw a line one inch (approximately 20mm) up from the bottom of the base and extend it on to all four sides. Cut a fraction above this with the No. 11 veining gouge. Then make a flute cut around the sides with the ½in (13mm) No. 9, using the lower edge of the veiner cut as a guideline. Note that the

reason the No. 11 veiner is being used, instead of the V-tool, is that it produces a rounded cut, better able to be blended to the shape of the No. 9 flute.

When wave-cutting you need to keep an open mind and to adopt a free-form approach, or the effect will look contrived. Try and convey the sense of power of the leaping dolphin and the disturbance caused to the water. Use whichever gouges seem best for the job. Take care not to create hollows too deep to be cleanly cut with the tools you have. For example, if you were to dig too deep, only a spoon-type gouge would be able to clear out the waste wood. Work with a twisting action. This will save having to apply much forward pressure, which could cause the blade to skate across the wood and damage parts already cut.

Throughout the whole of this project the graceful movement of this beautiful creature has to be paramount.

Fig 90   Project Three – completed dolphin.

9

Project Four
The Fish that Stands on its Fins

—————— YOU WILL NEED ——————

Suitable woods: Elm, Oak, Ash or Chestnut.
Minimum Block Size: Length 10½in (265mm); height
6¾in (170mm); width 4½in (115mm).
Tools:

¼in (6mm) No. 3	¼in (6mm) No. 6
½in (13mm) No. 3	½in (13mm) No. 7
¾in (20mm) No. 3	½in (13mm) No. 9
¾in (20mm) No. 4	¼in (6mm) No. 41 V-tool
¾in (20mm) No. 5	

Capturing a sense of movement will be assisted by using wood that has pronounced figuring, providing this runs sympathetically to the general line of the form. It is vital that the wood used is one of the timbers that has sound inter-cell bonding: use a wood that holds together well, like Elm. The reason for this is that there must be as little risk as possible that the wood could fracture in the area of the fins and tail, the most vulnerable parts of the carving on account of their relative slimness.

Unfortunately, as each year passes it becomes harder to find good supplies of Elm. Much of what remains after the ravages of Dutch Elm disease has become unsuitable, and can all too often show signs of decay, often proving too soft or pithy for carving. If you cannot find any worthwhile Elm, use Oak, Chestnut, or Ash instead. While with Elm it should be possible to provide the fish with reasonably thin and lifelike tail and fins, with some of the other woods it may be prudent to err on the side of caution and to keep these parts a little thicker and stronger.

PLAN FOR MOVEMENT (Figs 91–93)

It is essential to impart to the design a strong feeling of life and movement. This can be achieved in three ways. Firstly, the tail should be twisted, as it might be when a fish is constantly on the move. Secondly, the fish can be tilted, as if it were feeding on the seabed. Finally, the fish will stand on its lower (pectoral) fins, without the need of a plinth. For added support it can also be modelled to rest on the underside of its mouth, although this is seldom necessary.

Centre of Gravity

When the wood is just a rough block, it may be difficult to judge with any accuracy the probable centre of gravity needed to balance the fish. Clearly, this will have to be as far forward as possible, and certainly its perpendicular line will need to run through the pectoral fins. Consequently, it is important to get the angle of tilt right; if it is too shallow, the carving will be unstable. It is the depth of the timber (the 6¾in (170mm) dimension) which will govern the angle of incline the fish is to have, not the length. The length of the wood will be of secondary consideration. Do not, therefore, be tempted to design a fish larger, or longer, than the wood can reasonably accommodate. The angle of tilt needs to be at least 60 degrees. Plot this first, then design the fish around it. Stability will be increased if the pectoral fins are kept as long as possible. In the initial stages of roughing out keep them oversize. When the carving is nearing completion, and the true centre of gravity is known, they can be trimmed back.

Another vital factor for stability is the distance between the pectoral fins. When formulating the design, it is essential to remember that the outer edges of these fins need to take full advantage of the thickness of the wood. Consequently, it is best if the sides of the block are first planed smooth, and not left rough-sawn, before measurements are taken. Also, make certain the wood for these fins is totally blemish free, for it needs to be as strong as possible.

fin fluted or smooth

dorsal fin

fix final position
of Liquorice Allsort
eyes when head is
shaped

pectoral fin

cut away

fin surfaces may
fluted thus
or left smooth

anal fin

temporary block to be
removed when carving
is complete

Fig 91   Project Four – profile view, and data.

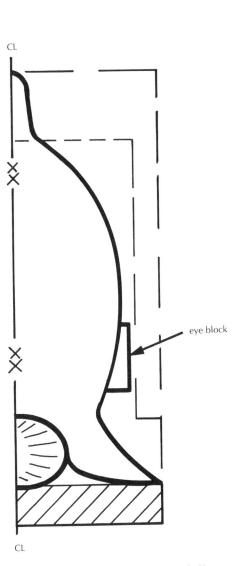

Fig 92   Project Four Front view – one half.

PLAN THE BODY WIDTH BEFORE CUTTING (Figs 94–96)

You will find it best to incorporate as much data as possible when the profile drawing is carbon-copied onto the wood. This will help to minimize the chance of errors. Around the outer edges of the block mark the planned body thickness, set in on both faces by approximately ½in (10mm), as shown by the hatched marking in Fig 94. This allows the pectoral fins the full block width. Note the area at the base of the fish

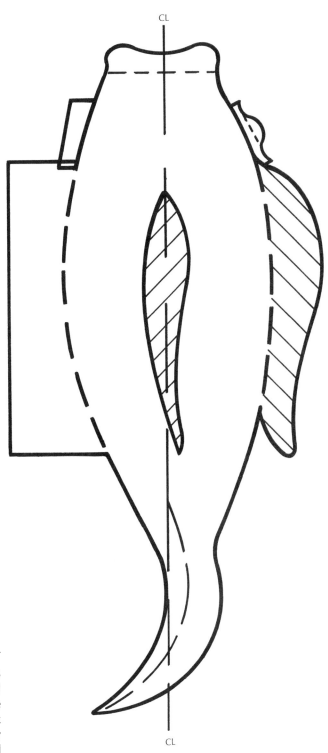

Fig 93   Project Four – plan view and approximate layout of main features.

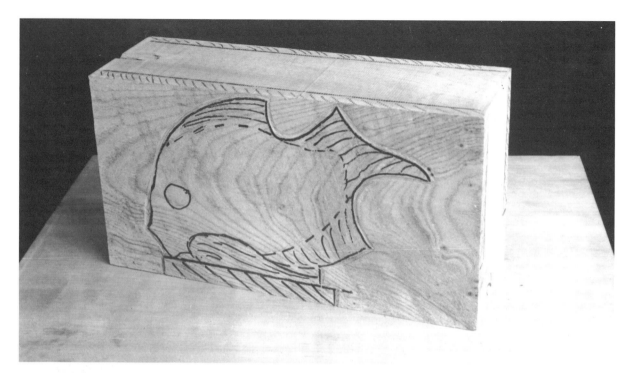

Fig 94   Get all the detail on to the wood.

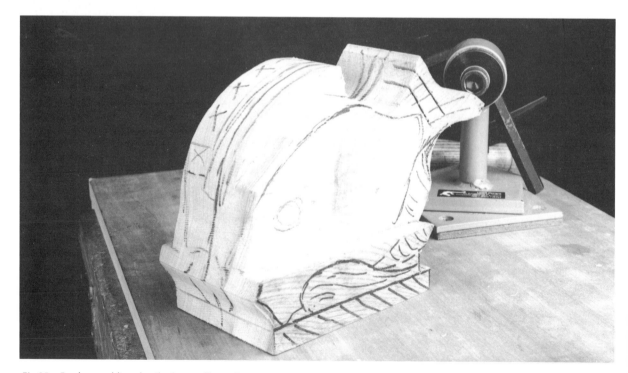

Fig 95   Re-draw, adding detail, after profile cutting.

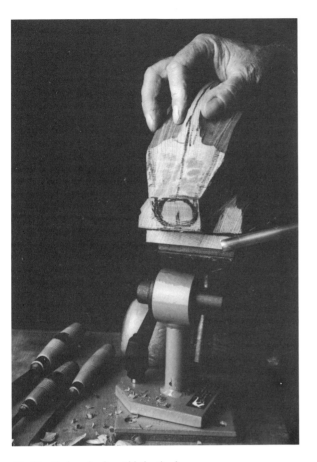

Fig 96   Reduce body width for the fins.

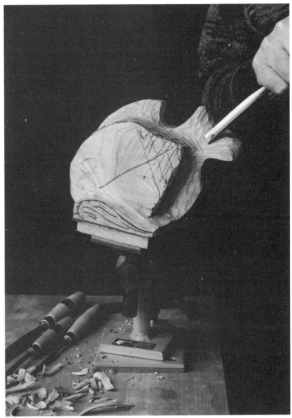

Fig 97   Gouge-cut leaving the fins oversize.

needed for screw-fixing the block to the workholder. The same amount of wood, or even a little more, would be required for holding the carving in a conventional woodwork vice. After marking up, and before sawing is done, cut round the design with the V-tool to give a small margin.

Once the profile shape has been cut, draw the frontal shape onto the wood. Clearly mark the wood to be sawn to ascertain the body width. When all the surplus wood has been cut away, the block form of the body and the spread of the pectoral fins will be similar to that shown in Fig 96.

SET THE SHAPE OF THE TAIL AND THE REMAINING FINS (Fig 97)

Roughly establish the shapes of the remaining fins – the dorsal fin on the top of the body and the anal fin on the underside – and the tail.

You may wish to curve the body, but remember that the bone structure of fishes is such that they can only wiggle the part from the dorsal fin back to the tail.

Work the fins and tail a lot thicker than they will finally be, allowing latitude for final adjustment. The more twist and curve you give to the tail the better the sense of movement will be. If possible, curve the tail to take full advantage of the run of the grain. This will give it more strength.

———————————— CONTOUR CUTTING (Fig 98) ————————————

Fashioning the tail is a classic example of contour shaping. The twisting tail can only be created by cutting with gouges that have steep sweeps. These will be those in the range of the 7–9 numbers. If shallow cutting tools are used persistently the tail will end up too flat. It is worth perfecting the technique, as it is bound to crop up time and time again, whether you are carving fishes' tails, folds of cloth or leaves; the method is always the same. The steep sweep of the 'quick-cut' gouges means that the corners of the blade edge are kept above the level of the wood. With shallow gouges they may very easily dig into the sides of the cut and split the wood.

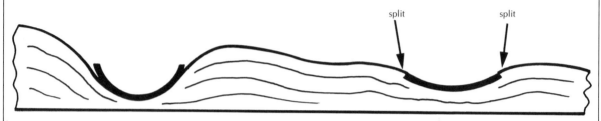

Fig 98   Corners of a shallow-cut gouge may cause wood to split.

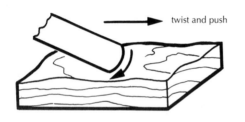

To improve contour shape, twist the blade as the cut is made. This does two things. It changes the angle of the cut and better presents the blade to a curving shape. It also means that the cut is made using a slicing action, similar to the way in which a guillotine cuts sheets of paper. More force is applied to a smaller area, producing a better, cleaner cut.

START TO SHAPE THE BODY

Begin by cutting a step around the fins with the ½in (13mm) No. 9 gouge. While the body area is still in block form, check that there is an even amount of wood on either side of each fin. This is particularly important where the dorsal fin is concerned. Then commence side-shaping, using light cuts with the No. 7 gouge followed by the ¾in (20mm) No. 5. Smooth off, using first the No. 4, and then the fishtail ½in (13mm) No. 3. Prior to gouge work, some saw cutting may be necessary to enable you to chop the waste out in small blocks. Take care not to saw too deeply here, or you will leave score marks on the body surface. The rear part of the body will need to be tapered down to the tail. It should be noted that the twist of the tail is carried back into this part of the body. Even the dorsal fin may well be curved, and part of it may lie away from the original centre line.

The body consists of convex curves running across and along its length. When removing surplus wood it is advisable to use shallow-cut gouges, as they will avoid the danger of digging too deeply. The ¾in (20mm) gouges are ideal, especially the No. 5, as their weight aids stability of cut and good tool control. It is essential to check the side-to-side balance by using your sense of touch. A side-view centre line also helps to even the balance.

———————————— SUPPORTING THE CARVING ————————————

If a swivel type workholder is used, like the one illustrated in the stage photographs, some support, or cushioning, may be necessary whilst the carving is tilted over on its side, otherwise the mounting screws may become stressed by excess pressure being exerted.

Fig 99   The pectoral fins need plenty of width.

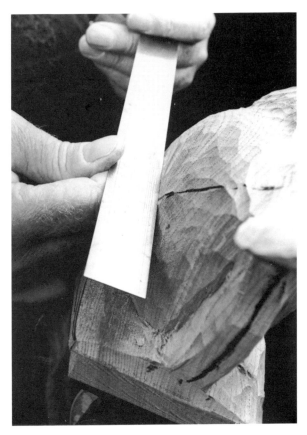

Fig 100   Check for flat spots with a straight edge.

STEP-IN THE PECTORAL FINS (Fig 99)

The body is narrower as it curves towards the under-side. This will lend added width to the pectoral fins. You will need to imagine parts of this shape, as the blocks needed for the fins will be obscuring it. Make the curve so that it looks as if it extends behind the fins, through to the belly of the fish. As the shaping takes place, be sure not to cut away wood required for the fins themselves. Keep the fin blocks level by cutting that area with the ¾in (20mm) No. 3.

CARVING THE EYES (Figs 101–103)

Before the eyes can be carved it is necessary to create as smooth a surface as possible; be sure no further shaping needs to be carried out. Smooth the wood as much as you can with the shallow-cut gouges, like

---

TIP

During body shaping, it is essential that compound curves are formed without any flat spots being left. It can be difficult to detect flats by sight alone, and it is best to use a straight edge, like a ruler, to check the curve. If flat spots are left they will become noticeable when the surface is polished, because light will be reflected differently.

---

the Nos. 3 and 4. It is tempting to start rasping straight away, but, in fact, gouge cutting is quicker and far more effective. Save the rasp till later, then, until you feel you have done all you can using the cutting tools.

Once you have achieved a reasonable degree of smoothness the eyes can be drawn in. I opted to use a stylized shape for my fish's eyes, which I felt was in

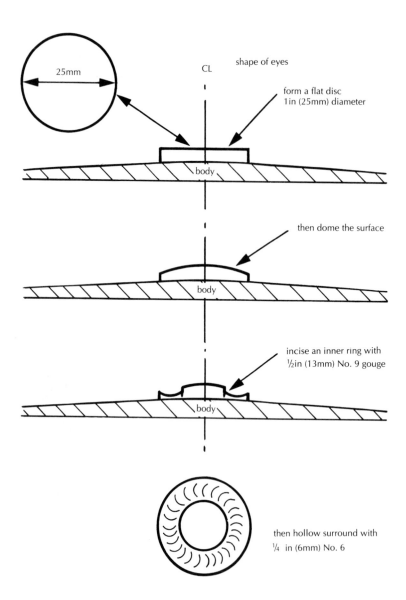

Fig 101   Project Four – eye detail.

keeping with the general look of the carving: they have an inner part as well as an outer ring, and look like old-fashioned liquorice sweets. The diameter of each eye was fixed at 1in (25mm).

Use the same method for ensuring correct eye alignment, as you did in Project One – that is, crossing the centre line on top of the body with parallel lines. These lines need to be extended down the sides. Draw in the first eye and then immediately match the second eye to it. If you do this without interruption

---

TIP

On any critical work, even a small error of alignment can mar the look, so it is really worthwhile taking plenty of care. I prefer to mark in the eyes, and then leave their actual carving for at least a couple of hours, if not overnight; coming back to the work with a fresh mind can work wonders – what seemed right the night before can look horrible in the cold light of the dawn!

you generally find you get a reasonable match without too much of a problem. If you need to take precise measurements, use calipers, or a compass, and a ruler.

Once the eyes have been drawn, chase round them just outside their periphery with the V-tool. Do not cut deeply, or you may find part of the wood needed for the eye will start to split away. Splitting, incidentally, tends to happen more often when cutting on an acute angle to the run of the grain. You may remember we covered this point before in the section on the owl's wings (Fig 52). However, it will be useful to go over this again. You need to be aware of the way the grain runs through the wood, and how, when cutting across it, the angle of cut is formed. If the angle is acute (steep) relative to the grain-run, then the tool will try to dig in, causing the wood to tear. When the cut is made on a shallow angle to the grain, however, the tool slides across the fibres, leaving a good finish.

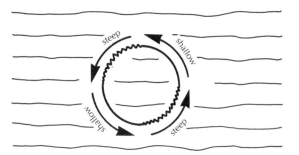

Fig 102   Eye shaping – cut on shallow angle of grain.

When forming a circle, like the outline of the eye for instance, you can expect two parts of the circumference to cut smoothly, and two roughly, unless the direction of cut is changed. Experiment on pieces of scrap wood and you will soon get to know when to change direction.

After incising the 'V' line, use the ¼in (6mm) No. 3 gouge to lower the surrounding wood. Do this carefully, or bits of the eye may break off. Use the same gouge to stab-cut into the incised outer ring to make it deeper. Trim to the drawn outline of the eye using stab cuts to maintain the round shape. Remember that there must be sufficient room between the eye and the pectoral fin to permit free passage of the gouge. Having pared away the surrounding wood, each eye needs to be given a dome shape. This can be done by

Once the circumference of the eyes has been fixed, you may wish to make small, but important, adjustments to the front of the head and the mouth. These need to be finalized before the eyes are completed. Use either the optional ½in (6mm) No. 6 gouge, or the slightly steeper cut No. 7 to give a slight upturn to the lips. This is also the time to remove any remaining felt-tipped pen markings. If these are left, they will prove troublesome at the finishing stage. From now on, use only lightly drawn pencil lines.

cutting with the ¾in (20mm) No. 3 gouge, used inverted. Alternatively, the dome can be shaped with the skew chisel. In either event, care is needed to ensure that none of the wood splits out. This is another instance where you will cut on a shallow angle to the grain. Give the eyes a light sanding to remove any minor humps.

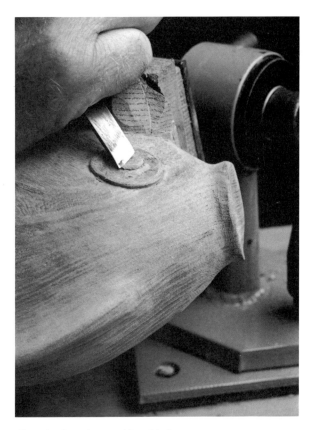

Fig 103   Round over with a chisel.

Once the domes are complete, the inner rings can be cut. There are two ways to do this, and in either case they need to be drawn accurately. Use a compass if possible. When I carved this project, I made the inner rings $\frac{7}{16}$in (10mm) in diameter. This meant that the circumference could be stab-cut with the $\frac{1}{4}$in (6mm) No. 6 longpod gouge. The other way to form the rings is to find a piece of tube of the right size, sharpen one end and use it as a punch.

If you wish, you can finish the eyes after this stage, but I chose to go one step further, and to create even more stylization. I left the inner part of the eye as a dome, but dished the wood between the outer edge and the inner ring, using the No. 6 longpod. This necessitated lowering the side of the concave near the inner ring by cutting a fraction of the wood away with the small No. 3 gouge.

THE MOUTH

If you refer back to Fig 91 you will see that a small area of wood has to be cut away from between the bottom of the mouth and the front of the pectoral fins. This can be done using a coping saw, or it can be chopped out with the $\frac{1}{2}$in (13mm) No. 9 gouge.

Draw the exact shape of the open mouth onto the end section of the carving, based on Fig 92. Make sure the symmetry of the outline is good, as you do not want the mouth to look lopsided. Use the No. 7 gouge to set in the shape of the pouting lips, which are best seen in Fig 93.

Carving the open mouth is best carried out with the work positioned so that you are standing directly in front of the fish, not looking at it from the side. In many respects, shaping the fish's mouth is similar to the way in which the snout of the pig was carved in Project Two.

Using the $\frac{1}{2}$in (13mm) No. 9 gouge, create a hollow to simulate the mouth being open and feeding. Avoid cutting deeply or you may experience problems clearing away the last of the waste wood. Cut in from either side of the mouth to prevent the edges splitting, and use the twisting action of cut previously mentioned.

THE LAST STAGES (Fig 104)

Little remains except to take out surplus wood from

Fig 104   Parts like this can be cut with a coping saw.

beneath the front of the anal fin. Cut this out using a coping saw, then blend into the body. Later, when the fish is free-standing and the length of the pectoral fins for stability is decided, this saw can be used for trimming.

So that the eye would not be distracted from perceiving the sense of movement, the wood was kept smooth. This finish permits the beauty of any natural figuring to be shown to its full advantage. With a plain and uninteresting wood, scales could be fashioned by stab-cutting their outline with a gouge like the $\frac{1}{4}$in (6mm) No. 3.

If you opt for the smooth finish, you may wish to add some decoration to the fins. In moderation, this will be fine, but avoid using too much embellishment. I chose to make a few 'V' cuts on the dorsal and anal fins, which was less than I had originally intended to do. More information on how this carving could be finished can be found in the chapter on finishing techniques.

If you have used a separate piece of wood to hold the carving in a carpenter's vice, or if the fish has been mounted on a workholder, now is the time for them to part company. I removed each fixing screw, one by one and, using a hard-back saw, cut through the wood below the pectoral fins. It is vital this is done accurately, so that the fish will stand level.

SHAPING THE UNDERSIDE

The underside of the carving – the bottom of the pectoral fins, and the part of the body between them – will need to be smoothed off. It is best if the fins are spaced apart with a division between them. This will mean carefully cutting a channel using the No. 9 gouge, after first drawing the shape of the fins, as seen from below. If you are at all nervous about doing this, then forget it, as a totally flat base to the fish is quite acceptable. Simply smoothing the bottom of the base will, though, still necessitate holding the fish upside-down in a vice. Protect the sides from being squashed and damaged with pads of rubber carpet underlay, or with kitchen sponges. Take utmost care – you do not want the fish slipping out of the vice and falling onto the floor!

Finally, check the centre of gravity. Move the fish backwards over the edge of the bench, or table, and see if any wood can be cut from the rear of the pectoral fins. Be cautious, and only take off the minimum amount of wood necessary. It will not do any harm if the fins are left quite long. Any tendency for the fish to rock can be cured by rubbing the base on flat sanding paper.

This carving was given an oiled finish, details of which are in the chapter on finishing techniques.

Fig 105   Finished carving.

Project Five
A Cat Called Puss

CONCEPT

For the third project depicting movement I recommend carving a standing cat. As you will recall, in an earlier project I mentioned that stylization may be needed to provide a sense of movement. To achieve this it is likely that you will have to exercise some artistic licence. For example, in this carving the length of the legs has been stretched to enhance the feeling that the cat is about to do something. All the time you are working you will need to keep the idea of movement very much in the forefront of your mind, if the resultant form is to be a success.

Let us look at what is required. The design needs to convey a sense of movement; it needs to look as if the cat has been captured on fast film when about to catch a mouse, or whatever, hidden from your view. The body has to have the look of being tense, as if the cat is ready to spring. The swishing tail is a flag to warn off other cats.

Much of the actual carving, to form the body shape for example, is straightforward. Consequently, to avoid repetition of the advice given in earlier projects, I have omitted detailing all the basic instruction, and have confined my explanations, in the main, to those parts of the carving where problems might occur. Some of the actual cutting will necessitate working in a confined space, such as under the chin, or between the legs, and, whilst difficult, this will prove an excellent learning experience.

THE DESIGN (Figs 106 and 107)

Whilst both the profile and frontal drawings are equally important from the point of view that one needs to know their shapes, only a copy of the profile will be used for cutting out the blank. I started by drawing the side view onto layout grade paper.

It is absolutely vital that, through to the modelling stage, the carving is worked oversize, as only by this means will there be enough wood spare in case adjustments need to be made to the posture. Such changes are bound to prove necessary if alertness and tension are to be conveyed. For example, at first sight it may seem from the drawings, and even in the photographs of the roughing-out stage, that parts of the cat – the paws, the ears and the tail, for example –

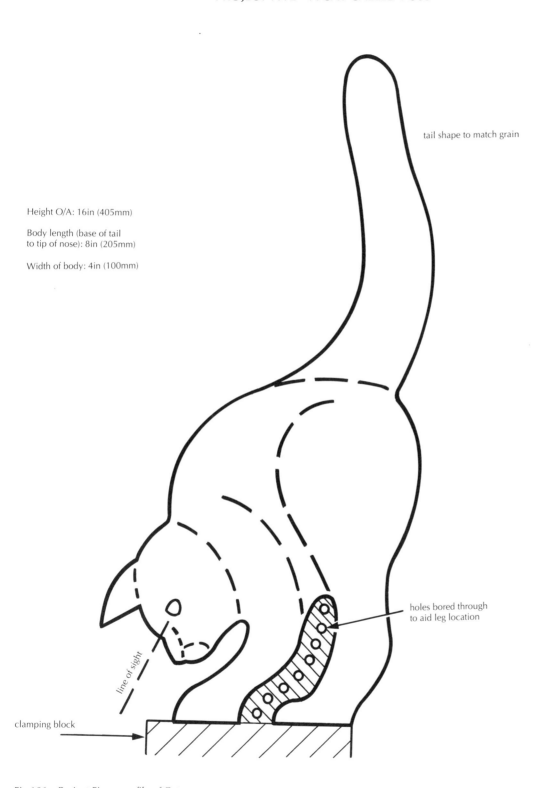

tail shape to match grain

Height O/A: 16in (405mm)

Body length (base of tail
to tip of nose): 8in (205mm)

Width of body: 4in (100mm)

holes bored through
to aid leg location

line of sight

clamping block

Fig 106   Project Five – profile of Cat.

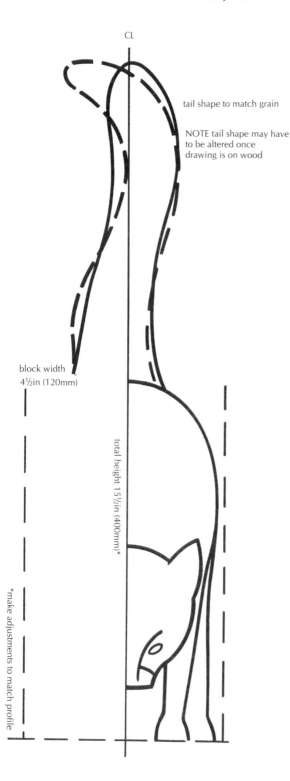

tail shape to match grain

NOTE tail shape may have to be altered once drawing is on wood

block width 4½in (120mm)

CL

total height 15½in (400mm)*

*make adjustments to match profile

appear larger than they need to be. This is intentional; they can be adjusted as the carving progresses. Working oversize like this guards against one of the most common errors – running out of wood. Do remember that having wood to spare in the roughing-out stage is like having money in the bank. You can spend it when you need to. In addition to those body parts already mentioned, keep the tip of the nose, as well as the mouth, oversize. You will need some latitude to model them.

The overall height of the carving was set at 16in (405mm). The body itself, from the base of the tail to the tip of the nose, measures a fraction over 8in (205mm), which matches well enough with the width of 4¾in (120mm), to give a stretched look.

Below the feet a block has been left so that mounting can be carried out conveniently, either in a conventional bench vice or by screw-fixing to a workholder faceplate.

Check that the Design Fits (Fig 108)

During the preliminary stages of fixing the design, it is really worth moving ahead slowly while making sure that both the side view and front view line up with each other, and being certain you are happy with the

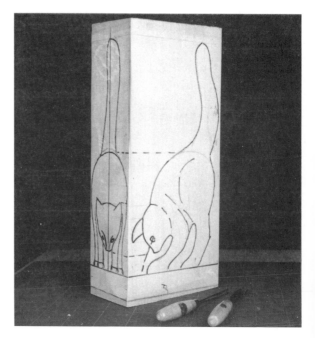

Fig 107   Project Five – front view of Cat – one half.

Fig 108   Outline drawings placed on to the wood.

general layout. First of all, carbon-copy the profile onto the wood. Strike locating lines from the main features and apply the front-view drawing.

At this stage the front view is only put onto the wood as a guide. Later, after the profile has been cut, it will need to be re-drawn freehand.

Centre of Gravity

The carving block has spare wood left at the bottom for mounting in a vice or onto a workholder. There are other reasons for having this extra wood: it will allow the hind legs to be extended if necessary, or the shape of the paws to be altered. It is also there so that adjustments can be made to compensate for the centre of gravity. This is similar to the way in which the centre of gravity was compensated for in the last project, when the fish stood on its fins. It is vital that the cat does not lean backwards, and it may well be necessary to increase the forward tilt of the work by adjusting the angle of the temporary base.

With the drawings on the side and front, stand the block upright. Check to see if the carving needs more forward tilt. It is vital to get the centre of gravity right. With the wedge of wood removed, there will be a forward incline, and the cat will tilt a few degrees, making it more secure (see Fig 108).

CUTTING THE WOOD (Figs 109–110)

With the possibility of modifications in mind, only cut out the profile. Do this using a bandsaw if possible.
- Draw the front view freehand onto the cut wood. (Use Fig 107 as a guide.)
- Mark up the main features and where the widest parts of the body will be.
- Rough-cut the shape of the tail, leaving plenty of wood for final modelling. Note that saw cuts around the tail should all end well above the body line, or their marks may show and be difficult to eradicate later.
- To locate the hind and forelegs, holes can be bored through the block from one side to the other using a $\frac{3}{8}$in (9mm) bit. A slot can then be cut with a jigsaw, working from both sides. (A coping saw could be used instead.)

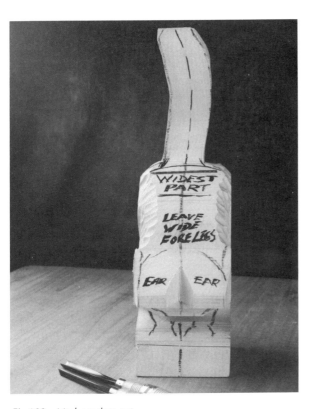

Fig 109   Mark-up then cut.

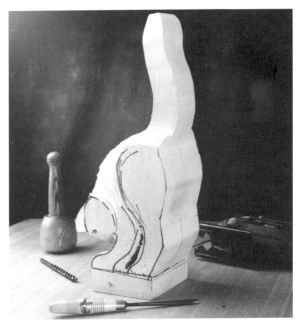

Fig 110   Drill holes then cut where the legs need separating.

ROUGHING OUT (Fig 111)

During roughing out, it is essential to keep both sides of the body evenly balanced. This means making sure features like the shoulders and the hind quarters occupy equal positions, and that similar amounts of wood are allotted to them. Check for imbalance both by sight and by touch. Once one section has been shaped, keep the carving in such a position, if you can, that you are able to see the part you have just carved while you work on the other side. This will help you to check the way the balance is progressing, and get a better mirror image.

TIP

The method by which the work is supported can make quite a difference to the ease with which you can work it. With a fixed, carpenter's type of vice, you may not have many holding options, and it may become difficult to position the work as just described and, without the facility to move the wood around, you could well find you have to twist yourself into an awkward posture. This is where a swivelling type of workholder comes into its own.

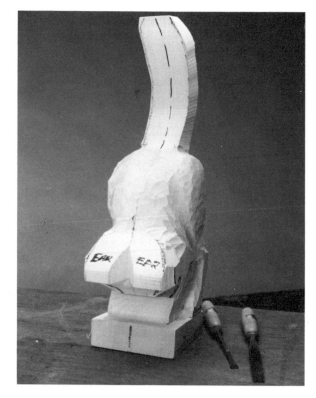

Fig 111   Step-in the front legs.

This stage is all about fixing the main elements of the design and getting rid of sharp edges. It is very similar to how the previous projects were carved, and it would be repetitious to go over all of the points again; just keep on the move – do not get bogged down for too long in one spot. There are one or two specifics, however, which require some comment.

• Angle-cut the face to form the cheeks, and notch midway across the width of the head to fix the centre of the crown. Also, at this stage, fix the approximate position of the ears.

• Note that the forelegs come closer together than the hind legs do; this helps to give the carving greater stability. Step-in the front legs.

At this stage, keep the front legs, below the head, as one piece. Do not separate them, yet, by cutting through from back to front, as this could limit their final shape and position, as well as weaken the carving.

• Once the position of both hind and front legs has been established, and marked with the V-tool, preliminary rounding of the body can commence. Use the ½in (13mm) No. 7 gouge for general body shaping.

For areas incorporating steeply shaped curves, change to the ½in (13mm) No. 9.

• Measure the distance from the top of the ear to the underside of the cheek, and transpose the same distance onto the other side of the face. The under-edge of the cheeks, running up to behind the back of the ears, is best cut using either the ¾in (20mm) No. 3, or the same size in a No. 4, depending on the actual curve which has to be made. Use the gouge to stab-cut the outline. This will help to ensure an equal shape to both sides of the head. Where wood needs to be taken off, 'plane' with the shallow-cut gouges, rather than using one with a steep sweep; this will give more accurate shaping.

THE FORELEGS (Figs 112 and 113)

Do not overlook the fact that the forelegs each have an elbow joint. They are one of the widest features, coming just within the width of the hind quarters. The elbow is approximately halfway between the base of

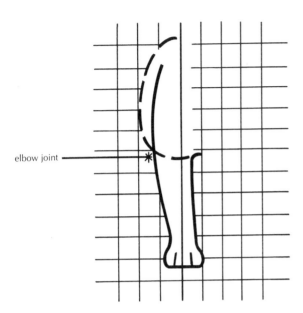

Fig 112 Foreleg elbow.

the foot and the top of the shoulder. From it the bones of the upper leg slope inwards to the shoulder blade. Below the elbow, the bones swing in to place the foot underneath the body.

It is important to get this visualization right, otherwise there will be a risk that the legs will look as if they just drop from outside the body. This may be perfectly acceptable if you are making a pantomime horse, not a cat! Just think of footprints in the snow, and how close together they are placed, each set coming well under the body.

As you shape the forelegs, you can start to develop the head by forming the cheeks with the ³/₄in (20mm) No. 3. Use the inside sweep to create the rounded shape needed, as well as for the shape of the brow of

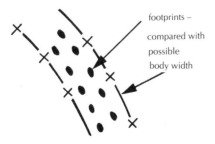

Fig 113 Footprints and body width.

the head. (For further details see the section on shaping the head.)

THE HIND LEGS (Figs 114–115)

Emphasis needs to be given to these, as they are dominant features, not simply merged into the body shape. Mark where you feel·the hind-quarter muscles lie, and make a light cut round the forward edge. Lead this down to the leg itself, using the ¹/₂in (13mm) No. 9. Make the cut on a shallow angle to the grain. Deepen it as the hind quarters are shaped.

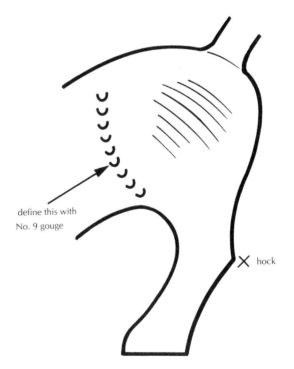

Fig 114 Hind-quarter detail.

The surface area of each hind quarter needs to be formed with gentle convex curves, and without any flat spots. Check for flats with a straight edge in just the same way as you checked the sides of the fish in the last project. Keep all the tool cuts shallow. Remember, the deepest cut made becomes the norm to which all of the surface area must be levelled. For this reason it is best to work the shape using the optional ³/₄in (20mm) No. 4, which is shallow enough to use with safety, but which will still remove reason-

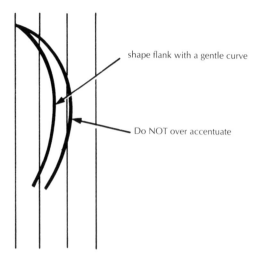

Fig 115   *Flanks to have gentle curves.*

Within the figure: shape flank with a gentle curve; Do NOT over accentuate

able amounts of wood. If this is not available, use the No. 3 of the same size.

Whereas the paws of the forelegs are close together, those of the hind legs need to be set wider apart. This will give stability to the completed work. When the hind-quarter muscle area has been shaped, the tops of the legs will have been drawn together somewhat, so that they fall under the flanks. This means that in order to space the feet correctly there needs to be some outward swing of the legs. This should start from the hock joint. Below the hock, the leg can be angled outwards slightly. Incidentally, note that the hocks are placed lower down the hind legs than the 'elbow' joints are on the forelegs.

As the legs are shaped, the side cut-away area between them can be enlarged. Do this using the ¹/₂in (13mm) No. 9 gouge, giving the tool a twisting action as the cut is made, to prevent it becoming stuck in the wood.

Separate the front paws from the back ones. Use the ¹/₄in (6mm) No. 9 to keep the gaps as narrow as possible. You should still aim to have the feet a touch oversize at this stage.

SHAPING THE HEAD (Fig 116)

It is best to carve the head in two stages, by doing the basic shape first, and following this later by the actual modelling. This method should produce a more realistic look; all too often, faces are carved flat.

During the first stage, concentrate on creating a spherical, or ball-like shape. Fig 116 shows how the three main view-points of the head – the front, the side and the plan – all fit into a common size of circle.

Avoid positioning the ears too close together; use thirds of the width of the head to calculate their size, as well as the space between. Start by cutting some of the wood between the ears using a tenon saw. Keep the saw cuts above the crown of the head, to avoid leaving marks. Remove more wood using the ¹/₂in (13mm) No. 7 gouge. Shape the ears using the ³/₄in (20mm) No. 3, with most of the cutting being carried out with the bevel facing away from the work, so that the shape of the blade forms the shape of the ear. To prevent the ears from looking as if they have been stuck on as an afterthought, create a small radius, using the ¹/₄in (6mm) No. 9, where they join the head. This will look much more natural than an angular joint would.

For accuracy, work the ears progressively. This means cutting a little off one ear, immediately applying the same cut to the other ear, then returning to the first. Switching from one to the other like this is preferable to shaping one ear completely, and then trying to match the other to it. Do not make the ears too thin, or they will become weak and may break.

As the head shaping develops, it will become necessary to work the underside of the jaw, and to access this you may have to do a little work on the shape and the position of the front paws. Eventually it will be necessary to pierce through between them, from back to front, but do not be in too great a hurry to do this. You will need to be quite certain that paw width and shape are correct. If you pierce through too early, there is a risk that the paws, and even the lower part of the forelegs, will be too slim.

CARVING THE FACE (Figs 117 and 118)

Even when looking downwards, the face is a dominant feature and it needs to be carved with care. The original profile drawing, Fig 106, provides sufficient space between the head and the front legs to give access for shaping the facial features. If you find any of the gaps too narrow, it may be that the legs need reducing, so make what adjustments you can before going any further.

The importance of shaping the brow cannot be overstated. It has to curve in two directions, from side

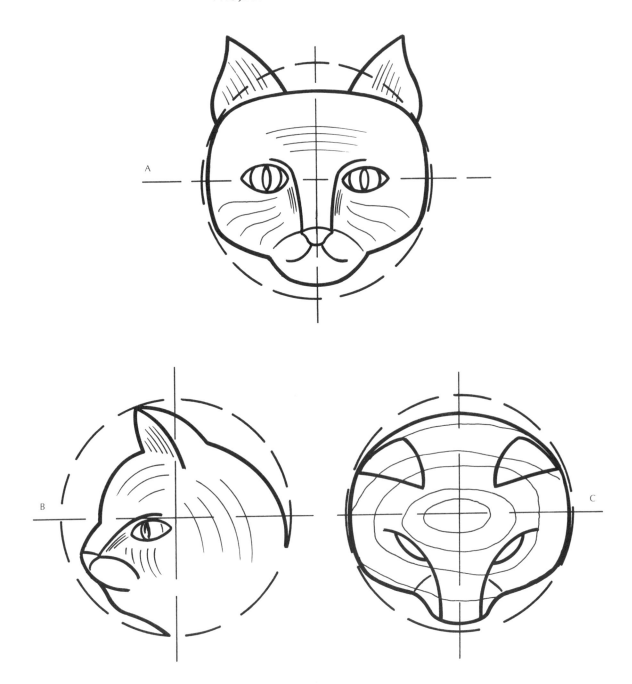

Fig 116   Head detail showing (A) frontal, (B) profile, and (C) plan view.

to side, and up to the crown of the head. Once you are comfortable with the shape, define the line along either side of the nose to the eye cavities. Make the marks lightly, using the V-tool. Next, form hollows where the eyes will be, using the ½in (13mm) No. 9 gouge. Use the same gouge to clear away any excess wood just below and to either side of the eyes. This will take the front curve of the cheeks back almost to eye level, as can be seen in Fig 117.

Use the ¼in (6mm) No. 3 gouge to cut back from

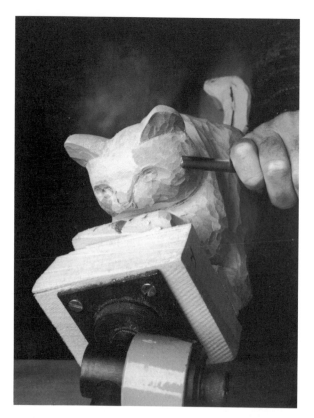

Fig 117   Define with hollows where the eyes will be.

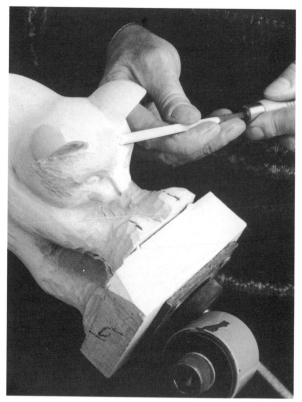

Fig 118   Use small cuts on the endgrain to prevent distress.

the tip of the nose, where the whiskers would be, and around the nostrils.

Although it should always be one's aim to work using the cutting tools, it may become necessary to resort to rasping, or to using coarse sanding paper, to achieve the contours of the face. It is certainly preferable to use these aids and be sure of a well-executed face, rather than battling with the gouges and making little progress. Having said that, do remember much of the contour shaping will be on endgrain. Rasps or coarse sanding paper will distress the wood fibres and leave scratch marks that will be hard to eradicate. In Fig 118, notice the difference between where the brow has been sanded and where it has been cut.

MARK IN THE EYES (Fig 119)

The eyes need to be drawn using vertical and horizontal lines, as described in the earlier projects, to make sure that they are correctly aligned. Do not

place them too far apart. Decide whether the outline of the eyes will be round or elliptical in shape. In either case the eyeball itself will be round. Stab-cut the outline.

Stab-cut using the ½in (13mm) No. 9 for a circular shaped outline, or use either the ½in (13mm) No. 6 gouge, or even the small No. 3, for ellipse-shaped eyes. Do not cut too deep. Proceed to the curve of the eyeball itself. Initially, this can be done using the ¼in (6mm) No. 3, using the inside curve of the blade, in the case of elliptical outline shapes; otherwise, the No. 2 skew chisel is a better tool to use, and certainly in either case for the final rounding.

To finish the eyes, make small, incised V-cuts at the centre of each eyeball to simulate the pupil. The cuts can be formed using either the V-tool or a small craft knife.

Once the eyes have been carved, check whether any excess wood needs to be taken from the sides of the cheeks.

Fig 119   Shape the eyes using the inside curve of the blade.

THE EARS

There is little point in hollowing the ears to any appreciable degree, since the indentations will hardly be visible when the cat is in its standing pose. It would also tend to weaken their structure, and deep cuts would be difficult to smooth. I made token hollows using the ½in (13mm) No. 9.

SHAPING THE TAIL (Figs 120 and 121)

The tail shape will provide an excellent opportunity to create the feeling of life and movement, so give it plenty of 'action' through its twists and curves. Use centre lines on all four sides so that you keep an even balance. Make certain that the tail really does grow from the middle of the rear of the cat, and not from one side. Whilst the tail of a kitten tapers to a point,

many adult cats have little or no width variation throughout the length of their tails, the tips of which are rounded.

Where the tail twists into a concave shape it can be cut with one of the 'quick cut' gouges, such as the No. 7, or the No. 9. For this type of shaping, many carvers prefer to use a round Surform rasp, feeling that this lessens the chance of them removing too much wood. Whilst this may be true, you will undoubtedly further your skill if you try using the gouge first.

There are, however, different ways to shape the convex parts. You can use an inverted shallow-cut gouge like the ¾in (20mm) No. 3, or you can round

Fig 120   Use a round Surform for the concave parts . . .

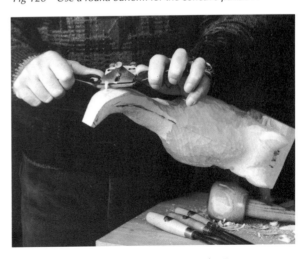

Fig 121   . . . and a spokeshave for convex shaping.

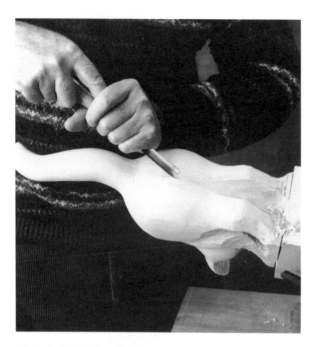

Fig 122   Start with a shallow gouge . . .

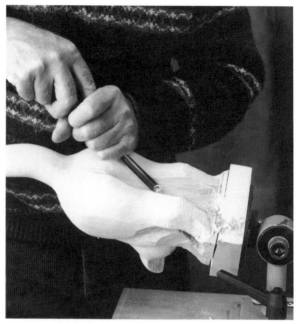

Fig 123   . . . and end with one that has a steeper sweep.

them using a chisel. Another tool you can use is a spokeshave.

Blend the base of the tail into the rear of the body with a gentle curve. At the same time, it is a good idea to finish off any shaping of the hind quarters and to separate the back legs.

FINAL WORK ON THE LEGS (Figs 122 and 123)

Cut any remaining spare wood from the back of the legs to form a hollow running down from below the tail through to where the legs separate. Width, and depth, need to be graduated, starting shallow and ending deep, by using different gouges.

Start by cutting immediately behind the hind quarters, using the No. 6 gouge then, as the trench deepens, switch to the No. 7 and finally use the $1/2$in (13mm) No. 9 for the deepest part. Where the legs divide, it may be tempting to drill out some of the waste, and to cut the remainder using a jigsaw. I prefer to use gouges, as drilling could inadvertently pierce the underside of the body. Work the cuts wider than the width of the gouge you are using; this will help to prevent it getting stuck. Leave the legs quite thick as they will not look so good if they are spindly.

Cut between the front legs whilst the carving is still on its mounting block. You might experience some difficulty in shaping the inside of the legs, as there will be little access for gouges. As the gap between the hind legs is opened up and the space between the front legs is enlarged, however, curved riffler files can be used. If you do not have any of these, shaping can be carried out using strips of coarse sanding paper.

FINISHING

It will be tempting to rush things, but try to resist. It is far better to check methodically whether any parts require further attention. Do avoid over-finishing the work, however. For example, it is a mistake to attempt to improve things at this late stage by making major changes; for one thing you will probably find that there is just not enough wood left spare.

The blandness of Lime can be improved by having a tooled, or textured-effect finish. This will also help to mask any dents or marks caused accidentally during the life of the carving, and that would show on a smooth finish. In the chapter on finishing methods, the technique of tooling is fully described. Briefly, it consists of making random cuts using mainly shal-

Fig 124   A Cat called Puss.

low-cut gouges, such as the small No. 3, or the No. 3 fishtail, and the No. 6 longpod. The chapter also explains ways of treating the wood prior to waxing.

Having completed this three-dimensional piece, we shall, in the next chapter, look at ways of reproducing designs on flat surfaces, and follow this by looking at how to carve in relief.

11

Finishing Techniques

Go to any art show where woodcarvings are on display, and you will probably see notices asking you not to touch the work. For fragile pieces, this is the way it has to be, but for sculpture it can be a mistake; people just love to touch and caress wood. At my own exhibitions, I always like to have a 'touch piece' near to the front, something not too delicate – like the Cottager's Pig – on which people can work off their enthusiasm. If the wood is well figured, so much the better; then people will be able to trace the wavy grain lines with their fingers. Wood is very tactile and people like to explore its shape. If the work is large they will walk all the way round it, and they will certainly stroke it as they pass. From this you will see that sculpture, or even relief work for that matter, has both to look good and feel good; if your work is at all lacking in either respect, the public will pass it by!

When I first started carving, I could never get my work anywhere near to the standard of finish I admired in other pieces. At one time I reckoned there must be some mystique about it all, and that only a talented professional could hold the key to success! In time I learnt there was no mystique, and that the only keys were experience and a good measure of perseverance.

There are various methods of finishing, and much that is written about the techniques concerns the treatment of flat surfaces, like those found in cabinet making, for instance. For treating carvings, however, the approach is somewhat different, although the basic ground rules of preparation still apply. In this chapter, the popular ways to achieve a good finish are described, and I have included a few odd wrinkles that I have hit upon over the years.

LIGHT REFLECTION

The way light falls onto wood, and is reflected back again off the surface, is clearly of considerable importance. In a gallery, obviously the look of the finished article can be greatly improved by the judicious use of lighting. Diffused light and spotlights can be used to achieve a desired effect when the carving is displayed. Light reflection is equally important while the finishing processes are taking place. So, firstly, let us give some thought to the question of workshop lighting, as this is something which is frequently neglected.

In workshop situations, the most common form of lighting is overhead fluorescent strips; while in the home, low-energy lights are gaining in popularity. The light from both of these sources is 'flat', and, while good as a background source, neither will show defects in wood, such as hollows or gash marks, as little or no shadow is cast. Shadow is needed if you are to detect hollows and bumps, and sundry mistakes. Also, shadow cast on to relief work will help to provide varying intensities of reflected light, which will enable you to see how the carving is progressing.

Apart from natural daylight, shadows are produced by standard tungsten-type lamp bulbs. Team up fluorescent lighting with a variable-angle desk lamp fitted with an ordinary filament bulb, and this will cast sufficient shadow for you to detect problem areas.

PREPARATION

While the technique used to finish a relief carving is different in certain respects to the treatment that may be applied to a piece of sculpture, they do have much in common, not least the degree of preparation required before the wood can be polished. It is a mistake to think that the surface of the wood will be improved simply by applications of wax alone; it will not happen, in fact, the reverse is more likely. The shinier the surface becomes, the more any defects will show. Before wood can be polished, it must be prepared.

Preparation normally takes the form of producing

an even and blemish-free surface. While in ordinary carpentry this can be achieved on flat surfaces by the use of power sanders, in the case of woodcarvings, much of the work has to be carried out by hand since few flat surfaces will exist. It is certainly tempting to rush through the various stages when sanding by hand, but do not. Initially, think in terms that it will probably take about the same amount of time to complete the preparation and finishing processes as it did to produce the carving in the first place. If that seems daunting, remember that, as your skill increases, things will get better – just a bit!

Preparation means, in simple terms, getting the surface into an even state, so that, when the wax polish is applied, the whole appearance is enhanced, not degraded. At this point it does not matter whether the final finish is to be smooth or textured. One thing is certain, however: throughout the carving of the subject, the sharper the tools, the better the cut surface will be. Sharp tools are a prerequisite to speedy finishing. They will leave clean, crisp cuts, not ragged ones that would necessitate a lot of sanding. If people start thinking your work has been chewed by the dog, you have a tool-sharpening problem to sort out! But

let us assume the gouges and chisels have been kept reasonably sharp, and that the wood is not too distressed. What next?

SCRAPE BEFORE YOU SAND

It always used to be the tradition to scrape wood before it was sanded. This could well have been because sanding papers were not as effective as they are today. Even with the good abrasives we have at our disposal today, it is certainly true that scraping – which is a cutting process producing tiny shavings – does remove unwanted material quickly and cleanly. It will also take care of any twisted grain that may be troublesome to cut with a gouge or tiresome to sand. You can scrape using glass, or buy specially made scrapers, or you can grind your own tools from old hacksaw blades.

Cabinet Scrapers (Figs 125 and 126)

Metal scrapers come in two basic forms – rectangular, and multi-curved, or gooseneck. It is worth investing

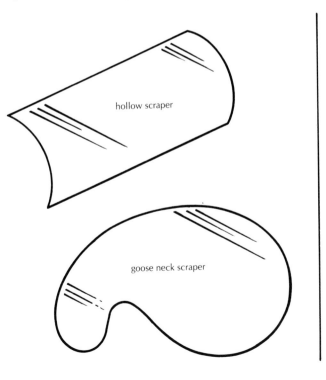
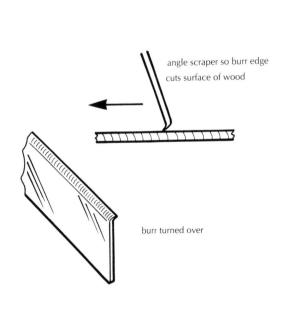

Fig 125   Cabinet scrapers and how they work.

TIP

Bits of broken windowpane work well as scrapers and although, surprisingly, you seldom seem to cut yourself, wearing strong work gloves is a good idea when using glass. Glass does not stay sharp for very long, however, and purpose-made metal scrapers are probably better in the long run.

---

in both types, although you will probably find that you will use the gooseneck type more often. Its variable curves go well with most shapes found in both sculpture and relief work. The scraping action is produced by a burr edge, similar to the roughness you create when honing a gouge or chisel. The burr is created by turning over the edge of the scraper using a hardened burnisher, or by dragging across it the back of a gouge blade. Many people find it easier to use a knife-sharpening steel, like those used by

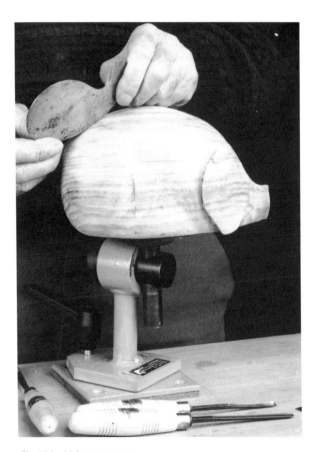

Fig 126   Using a scraper.

butchers. Another option is to use a small file. A few slight scratches may result, but they seldom seem to interfere with the final look of the wood after it has been sanded.

During use, the scraper has to be inclined to bring the edge of the burr into contact with the wood. Then tiny shavings will be produced, rather than wood dust. If you are producing wood dust at this point, try leaning the scraper over a bit more. To achieve a good finish, scraping needs to be carried out with the lie of the grain, or slightly on the diagonal to it. If you work against the way the grain lies, you will make the surface rough.

TIP

One element of any carving which benefits from scraping is endgrain. When endgrain is heavily sanded or rasped, the cell ends become dull and pitted. This becomes only too apparent when the wood is polished; it never takes a deep shine. Scraping, however, being a cutting action, prevents this from happening, so, if you have indulged in rasping, or used coarse sanding paper to help get the shape right, be sure to go over the wood with a scraper afterwards.

SANDING

Abrasives used for sanding have advanced considerably in recent years. Originally, they consisted of grains of sand (sandpaper) or particles of glass (glasspaper) bonded in a haphazard fashion to paper backing. Even today, you could still buy these types in any DIY store. Not if you want to finish wood properly, though: ordinary sandpaper will quickly clog and lose its abrasiveness; also, owing to the way the particles lie being random, they tend to leave scratches.

Abrasives work by wearing the wood away; they do not cut in the way a scraper does. When used properly, the modern types achieve excellent results, but to get the best finish you do need to know something about the various types which are available, and which ones to use for your carvings. Let us consider why one needs to sand at all.

Sanding may not always be necessary, and it is certainly true to say that if you need to sand you should only do it sparingly. Using coarse grades of abrasive should be avoided as much as possible, for they are no substitute for gouges. The only time this may not apply is when coarse sanding is being used as an alternative to rasping when shaping wood whose twisted grain cannot easily be cut, or where deep marks need to be removed for a totally smooth surface. Sanding should otherwise be confined to the removal of wood fibres which cause the surface to feel rough. Knowing how much to sand comes with experience; the skilled craftsman generally does far less than the beginner. One of the most important points to bear in mind is that excessive sanding will tend to obliterate fine detail. If your work is to have a crisp look to it, you will need to avoid excessive use of abrasives. This applies more, perhaps, to relief work than to sculpture. As a general rule, *avoid excessive sanding.*

Types of Abrasive

Abrasive sheets are made for a variety of purposes. The types which interest carvers are those made with **garnet**, **aluminium oxide** and **silicon carbide**.

• **Garnet** abrasive is very traditional. It is made from crushed garnet stone bonded to a paper backing. Like all other types of abrasive, it comes in varying degrees of coarse or fine grading. Garnet paper is reasonably long lasting and the coarser types are sufficiently 'open coated', with grains spaced out, to prevent too much clogging.

• **Aluminium oxide** has, over the years, become the most popular type of abrasive used. It can be used for hand-sanding and is in general use with power sanders. A wide range of grades is offered, the most common type being coloured red. There are, however, new types available (coloured blue, black and fawn), some being antistatic, to prevent a build-up of wood dust from clogging the abrasive face. Backing sheets of either paper or cloth are used, depending on specific applications. Because they are produced in controlled conditions, the grain particles are applied electrostatically to the backing sheet. This ensures uniformity, and avoids pinnacles that would cause scratch marks. Aluminium oxide is long lasting, and certain types are re-usable after washing.

• **Silicon carbide** is the hardest, and the most expensive, grit in widespread use. Its hardness is almost comparable to that of diamond, a quality which enables it to be used for sanding very hard

SUMMARY

- Buy materials from good and reliable sources.
- Use flexible paper-backed sheets and foam-backed pads for contour work. Use woven-backs when a stiffer form of sheet is needed, such as when shaping using coarse grades.
- For general use, garnet papers work well.
- For heavy sanding think in terms of aluminium oxide.
- Use silicon carbide types when lacquers have been applied.
- Woven pads are ideal for deburring and for rubbing in wax.

materials with compact surfaces, like glass and stone. It is also useful for sanding lacquer finishes and, in its finer grades, it is good for sanding wood after a shellac or cellulose sealant has been applied.

Grades of Abrasive

Abrasive grain is graded by passing it through mesh of various sizes. The **grit number** printed on the back of the sheet relates to the number of particles per unit area. It is an international classification, and the higher the number, the finer the grade. Grit numbers are either prefixed with a letter **P**, or followed by a **G**. For example, 80G grit is fairly coarse, 120 is medium, 240 grit is fine and, from 320 grade upwards, the grains of grit get finer still.

Types of Backing Sheet

The contours of most carvings will necessitate using flexible sheets of abrasive. Generally these are made of paper, but some of the woven backings are also quite flexible. Backings are graded from 'A' (lightest, for hand sanding) through to 'E' (non-flexible, for machine sanding). Less flexibility is obtained when the grit particles are resin bonded, although this type of abrasive is usually only used on a sanding machine, where more heat is generated than normal glue (usually hide-glue) can withstand.

More recently, abrasives bonded to foam sheets have been introduced. These are very flexible, and are ideal when contour sanding has to be carried out.

Another variant to straightforward sanding paper is pads of nylon fibres onto which aluminium oxide, or silicon carbide grains, are firmly bonded.

Fig 127   Sanding papers and web. (courtesy CSM Trade Supplies and Hermes Abrasives.)

They look similar to pan scourers, and are highly efficient.

Various types of abrasive papers and pads, with acknowledgement to CSM Trade Supplies and Hermes Abrasives, are shown in Fig 127.

PRACTICAL ASPECTS OF SANDING
(Figs 128–130)

You need to be as careful when sanding your work as you were when producing the carving in the beginning. Think about any edges or angles where you may be working, and try to retain their crispness. Remember that sanding a woodcarving is different to sanding normal woodwork; there will be few, if any, flat surfaces.

Use sanding sticks, rather than relying on finger pressure alone, in order to get the best result. You can make them yourself by covering pieces of split bamboo cane with soft leather like suede. You will need round sticks, as well as flat ones.

Unless you are carving a very large sculpture, you will do all your sanding by hand. This can seem a daunting task, but do not rush it. Abrasives work by the sharpness of their grains, and by their grit size, not by excessive pressure being applied, or by how fast you work the paper over the wood, so try and be methodical. Cut (rather than tear) your paper into small pieces. There is no advantage in folding it. In fact, the crease can crack the grit bonding.

To begin with, work over the carving using a quick-cutting grade, such as 120 or 150 grit. Use this to remove any blemishes you can see or feel. Do not leave them until the end, when only fine grade abra-

Fig 128   Sanding sticks.

sive is being used; it does not make sense to try and remove them using a fine grade paper. Work progressively through the grades, sanding with the grain as much as you can. It is never wise to sand across the run of the grain, as any scratch marks left will show. Sometimes, though, the shape of the work will prevent you sanding with the grain run. In this case, use a small circular motion, working the paper round and round.

When you reach the end of the sanding process, you may find that the surface is not quite as smooth as it should be. This can be a result of sanding with 'back and forth' strokes, where each alternate stroke lifts the grain fibres and makes the wood fuzzy. Avoid this by making the last few strokes follow in the direction which flattens the fibres and presses them into the wood. This process is best carried out using strips of sanding paper held by one hand and pressed onto the wood with the other. Just let the paper slip through the fingers of the hand pressing it down.

Some woods are more prone to fuzziness than others. Fibres can be hardened off if you wet them first:

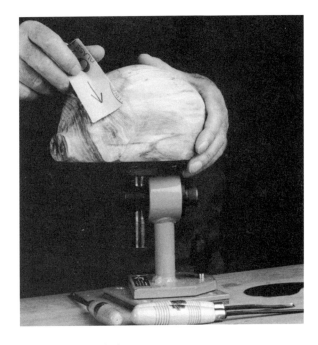

Fig 129   Sand with the grain.

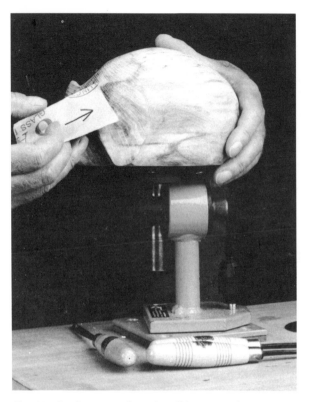

Fig 130 Sanding across the grain will leave scratches.

run cold water over the surface and let it dry, then lightly sand again (this is called **denibbing**) working as much as you can with the lie of the grain. Use only the finest of grit size, such as 500G.

Work under a filament light and examine your work critically. If there are any areas needing attention, go back to a harsher grade to clear them, then progress again through to the finer grit.

SEALING THE WOOD

When no further improvement can be made, the wood can be sealed prior to waxing. I never wax bare wood, as I have found the finish is better when a sealing coat has first been applied. Sealing can be carried out in a number of ways. These are the ones I tend to use:

• For light-coloured woods, I use either shellac sanding sealer, an acrylic sealer, or even a well diluted matt acrylic varnish. Shellac imparts a warm tone,

whereas acrylic will leave the colour of the wood virtually unaltered. Sometimes the choice will depend on whether or not the wood is to be stained. Sealing would follow staining and if a water-based acrylic stain has been used, then clearly, an acrylic seal should not be applied as it will tend to dilute the stain; in this case I would prefer to use shellac.

• Brown-hued woods respond well to an oil treatment. There are a number of finishing oils on the market. They all work in a similar way, and all require a number of hours' drying time. Oil can be applied by brush. Subsequent coats can be rubbed on using fine wire-wool or, if preferred, one of the newer web type pads. This will help to remove raised grain. The most essential thing about an oil finish is that the coatings must be put on sparingly. If they are applied too liberally, the oil never really has a chance to dry out completely, and it will remain tacky. When you apply oil, let it stand for a few minutes, and then wipe as much of it off as you can. The remaining thin film will then dry. After three applications, the wood will take on an eggshell sheen.

You can wax after the wood has been sealed, but a point worth remembering is that carvings, whether sculpture or decorative relief type, should never be so glossy that they look as if they have been varnished or dunked in treacle. Go for a sheen, not a shine. When waxing on top of an oil finish, make quite certain the oil is totally dry and hard before any wax is applied, otherwise you might find that the surface takes on a bluish bloom.

As far as the sculpture projects in this book are concerned, those pieces carved in Lime, such as the cat and the dolphin, received a shellac treatment; those produced in brownish woods like the Cherry used for the owl, or the Elm for the cottager's pig, were oil finished.

TEXTURED FINISH (Fig 131)

In sculpture, if the wood is well figured, a smooth finish will be the more appropriate. Never try and improve on nature. The look of bland woods, however, can be considerably enhanced if they are textured, by applying fine cuts. Invariably, relief carvings respond well to having a textured (cut) finish, on anywhere except 'high' spots which, because they need greater light reflection, should remain smooth.

Texturing can simply comprise random cuts, or it

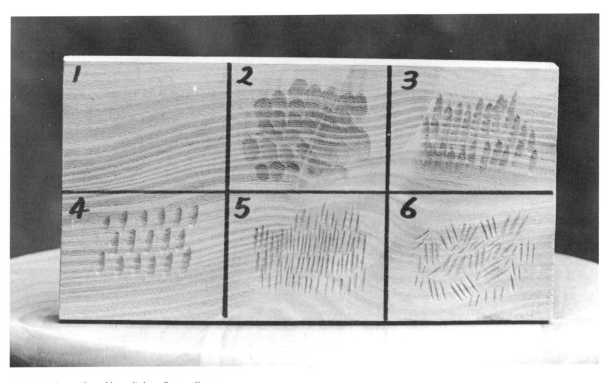

Fig 131   Examples of how light reflects off texture

can consist of cuts made in a more premeditated fashion to simulate, for example, fur, or feathers. If you decide to use a textured finish, try it out first on scrap wood, preferably of the same type as the carving.

This picture shows the effect of light reflection on the more common types of treatment. They are:

1 Plain sanded wood.
2 No. 3 gouge ripple cuts.
3 Inter-linked cuts made with a No. 9 gouge.
4 No. 9 cuts spaced apart.
5 Uniform V-tool cuts.
6 Random V-tool cuts.

12

Projects Six and Seven – Getting in Touch with Relief

Designs for flat surfaces, such as table-tops, need a different form of treatment to that used for panels and plaques.

INCISED CARVING (Figs 132 and 133)

A flat surface may need only to be carved with simple incised lines to provide decoration. These are cut using a V-tool, just like drawing an outline using a pencil or pen. If the surface is first given a sealing coat of, say, thinned varnish, the design can be darkened after cutting using a stain or dye without fear of

it 'bleeding' into the surrounding wood. This type of treatment is often used to decorate the tops of rustic-style coffee tables, using country scenes like a ploughman and his horse.

Where the surface does not have to remain absolutely flat, perhaps on a drawer front or a seat back, some elements of the design can be contour-cut, once the outline has been incised. Think of this as modified incised work. Part of Fig 132 is shown carved like this.

With modified incised carving you have the freedom to established contour levels to a limited degree. For example, the leaf centres, where the veins have

Fig 132   Project Six – a simple incised carving.

Little Owl, the subject of Project One, carved in cherry wood and finished with oil to bring out the bands of colour.

The author working on the Cottager's Pig (Project Two).

Working on the Cottager's Pig.

The use of weathered (spalted) elm added an extra dimension to the Cottager's Pig.

The Cottager's Pig – front view.

Using a gouge inverted to shape a wave in Project Three.

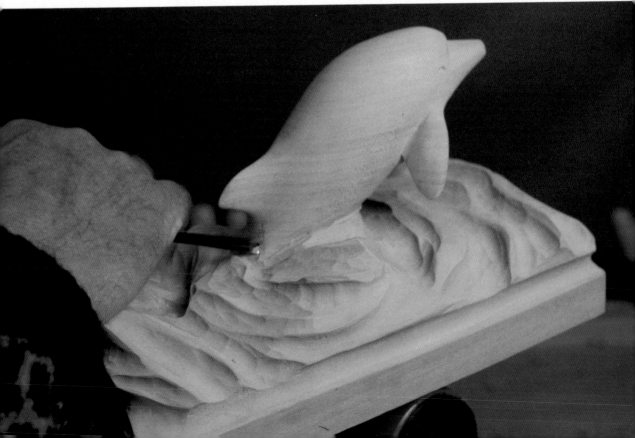

Waves with Leaping Dolphin was the subject of Project Three. It was carved in lime, finished with shellac and wax.

Compare the colour of the bare wood in this picture with the finished carving in the picture above.

Carving the waves – Project Three.

Project Four was carved in elm then an oil finish was used to enhance the strong grain lines to complement the shape of the fish.

This picture is typical of a carving in progress. Compare it with the finished fish in the picture above. Also note the diagonal centre line as well as the use of hatched lines to indicate wood to be removed or shaped.

Care is needed when shaping the fins to see they blend to the sides of the body without score marks being left by using a shallow-cut tool.

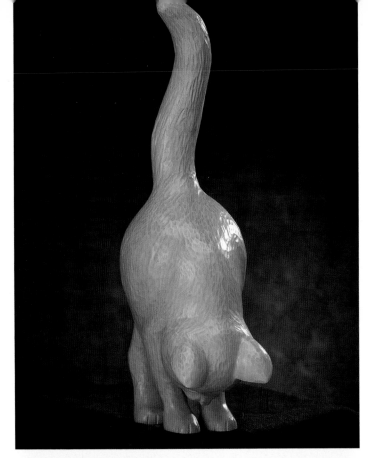

Project Five. Note the tooled finish. If the wood used for this piece (lime) had been left smooth, it would have looked bland and the carving could have lost some of its visual impact.

Low relief carving of a Wild Rose, in cherry wood, detailed in Project Seven.

Project Seven. Showing how the background was removed with a 'quick-cut' gouge.

Shaping the flames of the Sunburst with a broad-bladed gouge.

The Sunburst – Project Eight – was carved in bland lime, then coloured to give this warm, bronze look.

The Mirror Frame in Project Nine was carved from light-coloured chestnut. When finished the frame was darkened by fuming to produce a warm tone.

Note the supporting blocks visible inside the cut-out, used to secure the carving to the backing board.

Experimenting with shapes of bases. The one used in Project Ten is on the right of the picture.

Front row: A Cat called Puss (Project Five); Wild Rose (Project Seven); The Fish that Stands on its Fins (Project Four); Blackbird (Project Ten); Mirror Frame (Project Nine); Dolphin (Project Three).
Back row: Sunburst (Project Eight); The Cottager's Pig (Project Two).

In this carving (Project Ten) the visual contrast between the blackbird and the base has been expanded by the bird having a smooth finish, while the leaves and branches are tooled.

use mirror image for right side
if only cutting outline prior to
staining

hollow if required

Fig 133   Project Six – incised carving.

been cut, are at the original surface level, yet there are depressions on either side.

PROJECT SIX

Making Incised Cuts (Figs 134–136)

Try using the simple incised method to cut the outlines of the designs.

Use any wood which can be easily cut, like Lime or Sycamore, or perhaps even plantation-grown Mahogany bought from a reputable source. Hold the pieces in place using a backing board (*See* Fig 141, Project Seven), or in the bench vice.

Fig 134 offers you two alternatives; you can use it, as shown, simply to incise the outline (left), and to work some of the design (right) in the modified manner or, if you prefer, you can produce the whole design in either or both techniques. Simply reverse the copy of the drawing and use the image from the back to make up a complete design. To colour the outline, seal the wood first before carving, using either matt acrylic varnish or sealant, diluted with a little water, or apply a coat of matt polyurethane varnish, thinned with white spirit. After cutting, run some wood dye into the cut lines, dabbing it off where it spreads onto the flat surface of the work.

Transfer the drawings onto the wood in the usual way using carbon paper.

Cut the outline of each design using the $^{1}/_{4}$in (6mm) No. 41 V-tool. Try and leave small gaps where lines meet. When using the design shown in Fig 134, hollow either side of the central veins with the $^{1}/_{4}$in (6mm) No. 6 longpod.

Fig 136 shows the same design as that shown in Fig 134 but carved in **low relief**.

Of the various types of decorative treatment, low

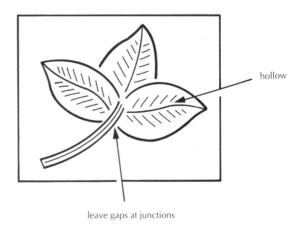

hollow

leave gaps at junctions

Fig 134   Project Six – modified incised carving.

Fig 135   Leaves cut using the incised method.

Fig 136   Leaves in low relief.

relief is probably the most popular. The other treat-ment, high relief, is preferable when greater emphasis of depth is required. The potential of relief work should not be ignored by anyone new to carving. Not only does it permit designs to be worked which might otherwise be unsuitable for three-dimensional execu-tion, but it will certainly help the beginner to under-stand much better the make-up of wood, and how it can or cannot be cleanly cut, and, last but not least, how necessary it is to work with razor-sharp tools. The reason is that in three-dimensional carving you can take liberties. You can rasp and you can sand with coarse abrasive to create shapes or get rid of badly cut wood. There is not, strictly speaking, much scope for these indulgences when you are working in relief, however, if you want crisp carvings; they have to be cut using sharp tools and you need to learn to feel the way the wood wants to be cut; you cannot dominate it. There is an added bonus, though; relief work can be combined with sculpture to bring out detail and to add interest to the piece. Learn how to carve in relief and you will expand your horizons.

PROJECT SEVEN

Wild Rose in Low Relief

It is best to begin by working in relief to a depth of around ¹⁄₂in (about 10mm). If you try to make your work shallower it will become more exacting, as there will be less tolerance for correcting mistakes.

YOU WILL NEED

Wood: The wood I recommend using for this project is native Wild Cherry. Alternative timbers could include Lime or Sycamore. The piece of timber should mea-sure 7⁷⁄₈in (200mm) wide, 11³⁄₄in (300mm) long and 1in (25mm) thick. Plane on both faces to an equal thickness.

Tools:

³⁄₈in (10mm) No. 2 skew	¹⁄₂in (13mm) No. 6
¹⁄₄in (6mm) No. 3	³⁄₁₆in (5mm) No. 7
¹⁄₂in (13mm) No. 3 fishtail	¹⁄₂in (13mm) No. 7
³⁄₄in (20mm) No. 4	¹⁄₄in (6mm) No. 9
³⁄₄in (20mm) No. 5	¹⁄₈in (3mm) No. 11
¹⁄₄in (6mm) No. 6 longpod	¹⁄₄in (6mm) No. 41 V-tool

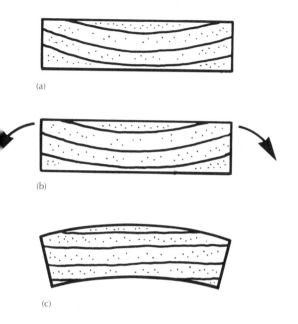

(a)

(b)

(c)

Fig 137   How wood distorts.

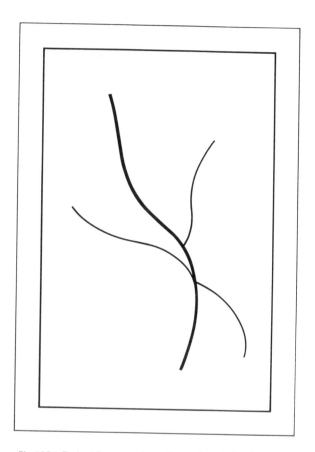

Fig 138   Project Seven – primary/secondary design lines.

Fig 137 shows typical sawn timber. 'A' shows which way up the annual rings should be, when viewed end-on. Note that the rings curve upwards. The top surface was the side of the wood nearest to the tree's centre. The reason for this is that, as the wood stabilizes, the natural tendency of the rings is to try and flatten out, as shown in 'B', causing the surfaces to distort. This can happen even when the wood is seasoned. Any bowing, as shown in 'C', is less noticeable than when the opposite (cupping) happens. Always check which way up your timber is before you apply the drawing.

Drawing the Design (Figs 138 and 139)

Fig 138 shows the starting point of the design. Curved shapes have a more natural look; apart from being easy on the eye, they are more true to life than straight lines and sharp angles.

When producing the drawing, the following points needed to be taken into account:

• It is vital that all the gaps between the leaves and stems are sufficiently large to accept the width of the tools to be used. This may seem an obvious remark to make, but believe me it is not at all uncommon, even for a skilled craftsman, to overlook the fact you have to get tools into narrow gaps! So, before doing any-

thing else, check the widths of your gouges to see they will fit. If, incidentally, you are using the sizes mentioned, including the optional ones like the $^3/_{16}$in (5mm) No. 7, then you should have no difficulty. Should you be in any doubt, alter the design.

• The stems should have a gradual taper. The dotted centre lines will help to avoid slimming them in the wrong places, which could make it look as though the plant is dying. It is best to draw the stems thicker than their size will eventually be. Remember – spare wood is like money in the bank!

Clamping the Carving Wood (Fig 141)

You will need to hold the carving wood securely, yet at the same time you need to be able to change its position easily. As the work develops, you will want to be able to look at it from time to time with the panel standing upright, so that you can see how the

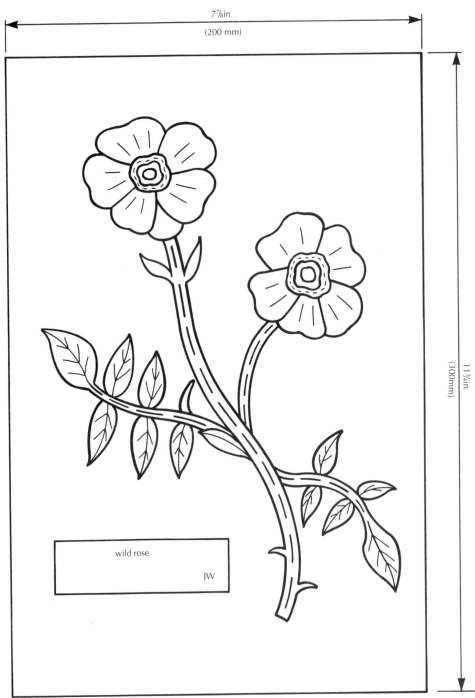

7⅞in
(200 mm)

11¾in
(300mm)

wild rose

JW

1in (25mm) prepared cherry

Fig 139   Project Seven – Wild Rose.

Fig 140   Project Seven – showing drawing fixed to wood, V-tool and mallet.

shadows are cast. For ease of handling, I find the following arrangement works well, and it costs virtually nothing. Firstly, you need a backing board, about ³⁄₄in (approximately 20mm) thick. This needs to be larger than the panel to be carved. Use plywood, chipboard, or MDF (medium density fibre-board), any of which you should be able to buy cheaply as off-cuts. Use four strips of wood, which need to be thinner than the carving wood itself. With the carving wood in place on the backing board, fix the strips, around the carving, to the backing board using panel pins. Have them fitting reasonably tightly, while still being able to remove the panel. Hold the backing board to your bench using G-clamps.

Mark in the Background Depth (Fig 142)

Before starting to carve, mark the planned background depth onto the sides of the wood. In this example, a depth of ¹⁄₂in (10mm) was used. Draw a bold line, and then just above it a dotted line. The space between the two lines acts as a safety net. Initially, all cutting is carried out to the depth of the dotted line. After the bulk of the waste wood has been removed, and the modelling stage has been reached,

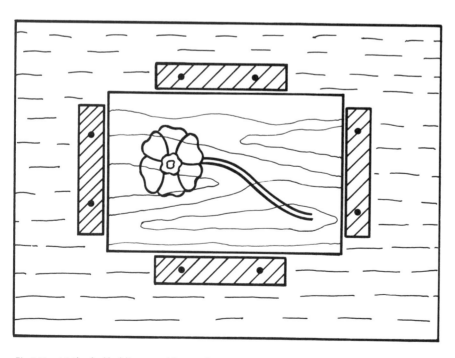

Fig 141   Method of holding wood for carving.

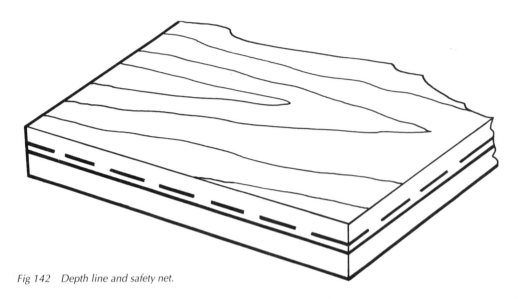

Fig 142   Depth line and safety net.

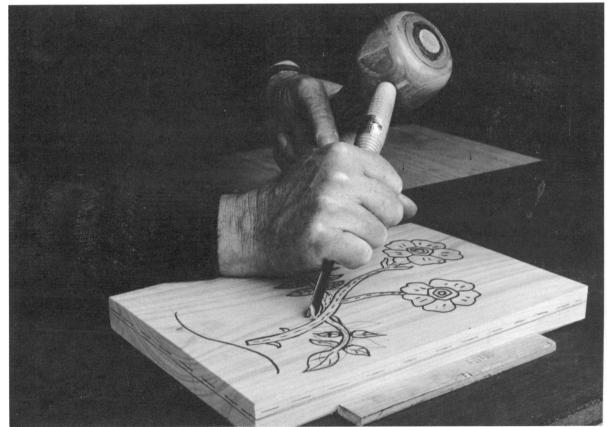

Fig 143   Using the V-tool and mallet to cut a trench around the design.

the wood can then be trimmed back to the final line. Working like this ensures no unsightly marks should be left on the background surface.

Second Safety Net (Fig 143)

The next step is to cut a shallow trench around the design. This forms your second safety net, and is there to prevent the design itself being cut away by mistake whilst the background is being reduced. Another reason for this safety zone is to alleviate stressing the wood as stab cuts are made. We shall return to this point later on.

For cutting the trench, use the V-tool, just as you did in the incised work. This time, though, line up one corner of the blade on the design. The trench will then be cut just outside the design perimeter. Where there is tiny detail, like the small leaves, cut round them all together in one block.

Background Removal

You can use either of two methods to reduce the background: it can be done by cutting, at right-angles or diagonally to the grain run, using a gouge like the ¼in (6mm) No. 9. This size and sweep will remove waste wood quickly. If you keep the corners of the blade just above the level of the wood the cuts will be clean, not ragged. You need to work progressively over the whole of the background, using light cuts rather than trying to dig deeply into the wood. Note that at this stage it is only necessary to cut up to the incised trench. Use the No. 9 gouge until just a shade above the dotted safety line.

TIP

Unless otherwise stated, it is assumed you are looking at the carving as it lays flat on the bench. So, the phrase 'cutting the high parts' means 'those parts which stand out furthest from the background', not the parts of the design at the top of the panel.

If you own a router you can use it with a flat-bottom cutter to remove much of the waste. Be careful not to cut too deeply. Some scrap wood of the same thickness as the carving will be needed to prevent the router from tilting when you reach the edges of the panel. To avoid a machine-cut look with a very even surface, set the depth gauge higher than the safety net depth, then the last of the wood can be removed by gouge-cutting. This will retain the 'hand-finished' look.

Whichever method is used, take off the last of the wood to the depth of the dotted line using shallower cutting gouges. For this project I used mainly the ½in (13mm) No. 7, followed by the ¾in (20mm) No. 5, and the No. 3 fishtail. There may be parts of the waste wood left, which you cannot clear using these gouges; they can be removed during the next stage. Try and keep the background as even as you can. Invariably, it tends to rise up the nearer you get to the design. Use your sense of touch to detect high spots.

Trimming the Design (Figs 144–147)

During the trimming stage, the design can be kept at its original thickness. This means that when trimming is complete the design should have sides at right angles to the background. The only exceptions may be intricate areas of detail, such as the smaller leaves. For these, some contour shaping may be needed before it is possible to access between the gaps to remove waste wood.

You need consciously to retain the vertical sides of the design. If by mistake they are allowed to incline inwards or outwards it will affect the shape of the design once contour cutting starts. Clearly, if the original surface is lowered and the sides are not at true right angles, the shape will get either smaller or larger depending on which way the sides slope. Fig 144 shows how angle-cutting can (a) reduce, or (b) enlarge the design shape, whereas vertical sides (c) leave the shape unchanged.

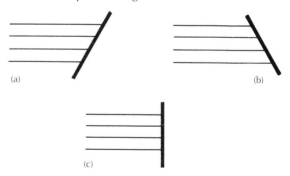

Fig 144 Cuts (a) and (b) show the effect of not making a true downward cut as in (c). Angled cuts affect design width.

Fig 145   Making trimming cuts. Note that the gouge leans away from design, then bevel-cuts vertically.

You need to be aware of the way the blade is being applied to the wood when making downward trimming cuts: if the inside curve of the gouge sweep is facing the design, and the bevel is outwards, hold the tool *upright*; when the bevel is towards the design, angle the blade *outwards* to allow the bevel to make a vertical cut.

Work round the design, holding the tools whichever way you have to, to ensure all the sides are kept as near vertical as possible. Cutting between the small leaves may prove difficult. If so, you can wait until they are contour-shaped and lowered, and then there will be less wood to contend with. This may entail some re-drawing to retain their shape and position. Cutting between the leaves can be done using the No. 11 veiner, but take care not to apply too much pressure. Where possible make the gaps 50 per cent wider than the tool being used.

When making trimming cuts, be aware of two fun-damental points. (You may recall these were covered in the early sculpture projects.)

• Do not stab-cut with the run of the grain unless a stop cut has first been made across the wood. If you forget to do this, you could easily split the design.

• Do not stress the wood by making forceful wedging cuts near to the design itself when waste wood is still present. Always trim back in stages, with the first cut made well in the waste, the next one just inside the waste, and the third cut close to the design line.

Stems and Leaves (Fig 148)

With many plants, where a sub-stem meets the main stem, the point of junction forms a small radius, not a sharp angle. Use the veining tool (No. 11) to make these rounded cuts. Another thing to consider is from what point the sub-stems grow out from the main stem: you could show them growing from the side,

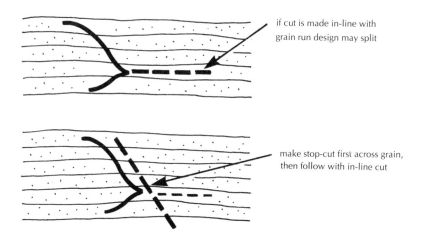

if cut is made in-line with grain run design may split

make stop-cut first across grain, then follow with in-line cut

Fig 146   Cut across the grain before you cut with it, or the wood may split.

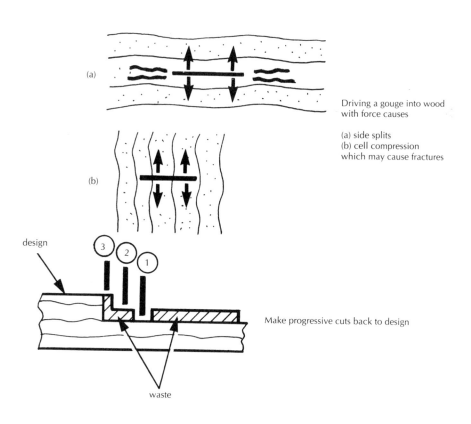

(a)

(b)

Driving a gouge into wood with force causes

(a) side splits
(b) cell compression
which may cause fractures

design

Make progressive cuts back to design

waste

Fig 147   Avoid 'wedging'.

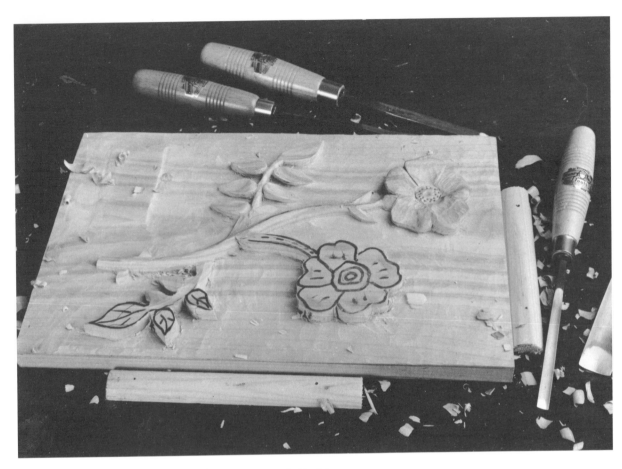

Fig 148   View of sub-stems and leaves. Also texture cuts to finished flower.

coming from behind, or possibly from the front; choose which you prefer. Try to introduce some variety when more than one stem is involved.

Leaf-Stems May be Too Small to Carve

I chose to fashion all but the main leaves directly onto the sides of their stems, without their own specific leaf-stems, because of the relative small size of the joints. Outline shapes were made using the ¼in (6mm) No. 3 gouge. These needed to be done close to where the leaves and stem met, so only very light cuts were used to stab. They were later deepened to allow each leaf some curl when their shapes were finally modelled.

Modelling (Fig 149)

Much of the success of relief carvings is owed to the way in which light is reflected off the wood. The more variation there is in the surface treatment, the better the result will be. For example, if the main areas are flat, light reflection will be minimal, and the carving will remain dull and uninteresting. To achieve a lifelike appearance, there needs to be plenty of contour variation. This will mean making full use of the design depth, and to do this you will need to know which are the high spots and where the low points occur. Clearly, the best way to get to know the contours is to go and look at a real wild rose or, failing that, at some good photographs.

When new to carving, people find it difficult to visualize contour shaping. One way to overcome this is to use different colours of chalk to show the differ-

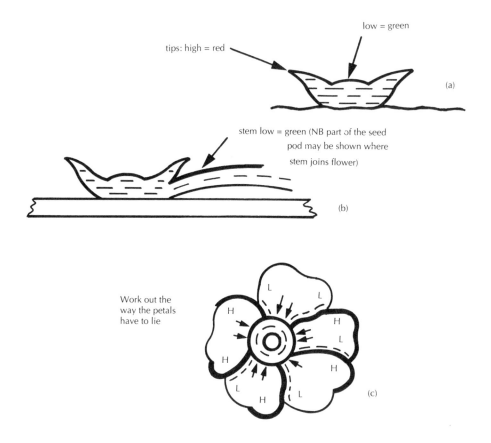

low = green

tips: high = red

(a)

stem low = green (NB part of the seed
pod may be shown where
stem joins flower)

(b)

Work out the
way the petals
have to lie

L   L

H

H   L

H   H

L   L

H

(c)

Fig 149   Use of colours helps to plan contours.

ent levels needed. In effect you use the same process as any map-maker would. Low areas can be marked green; high spots red, with those levels in between blue or brown, perhaps.

Let us take two simple examples.

Think of the centre of the flower: is it to be set low, with petals cupping around it, or is the centre high, with the petals folding back? If you opt for the first choice, as shown in Fig 149a, then you would mark the centre green for low, and the tips of the petals red, these being high points. If some petal tips roll over, or dip down, they would need to be marked with the mid-range colour.

Let us look at the main stem, as shown in Fig 149b. It has to appear to go to the back of the flower, so, just before the petal tips start, the stem has to be low. Mark it green.

Spend some time making sectional drawings. These will help you to come to terms with contour shaping. Look at the main flower drawing again. Some of the petals are positioned on top of others. You will need to mark the dominant edges, as seen in Fig 149c, and where the first cuts will be made.

Once you have a perception of the shapes you need you can, if you like, apply the colours to the wood itself.

The Need For a Centre Line

While the human brain is perfectly happy to accept designs which may not be realistic, it will immediately reject simple errors of alignment, even when they are so slight we may not notice them straight away. In other words, you can look at something and know it is not quite right, even if you do not know why. A common mistake in foliage carving is not getting the flower stem lining up properly with the flower centre; it only has to be out of true by a fraction to look wrong.

Overcome problems of alignment by the meticulous use of centre lines. Lightly draw the lines along the stems through to the very centre of each flower. It is also advisable to do the same with the main leaves. Be sure to replace the lines as they get cut away.

Where to start Carving

Once you make a start you will find that modelling the work becomes easier to understand. A basic rule of all relief carving is whenever possible to establish the low-lying levels first, before working on the higher ones. Then you will be more likely to manage all the relief work within the prescribed depth. If you try and work the other way round, forming the 'highs' before the 'lows', you will invariably find you have to make the depth line deeper, or, worse, you will just run out of wood!

Make your first modelling cuts close to where the main stem goes behind the flower. Do this by stab-cutting just outside the flower shape using a broad gouge like the ¾in (20mm) No. 4. Then, reduce the stem depth. Keep the angle of cut steep; you can always lessen it later. In case you are wondering why the first cuts are made using a broad gouge, the reason is that the weight and size will give you more stability which, in turn, will produce a confidently positive cut. Try doing it using a small gouge and the result may not look so good.

Once that part of the stem has been lowered, take out the centre of the flower to just above its final depth. To do this you will have to make a ring of light cuts. These will be made deeper once some of the waste has been removed and the possibility of stress has been reduced. Use either the ½in (13mm) No. 6 or the No. 7 to cut the ring, depending on the size of the centre. Remove the waste using the ¼in (6mm) No. 3. The centre can then be slightly domed by dipping its outer edge using the inverted No. 3 gouge and then rounding over it using the No. 2 skew chisel.

Setting in the Petals (Figs 150 and 151)

Follow the centre shaping by stab-cutting the petals, using Fig 149c as a guide. The gouges to use will depend on the actual shapes you want for the petals. In my example, much of this work was carried out using the ¼in (6mm) No. 3 gouge for the smaller

shapes, and the ½in (13mm) No. 3 fishtail for the larger ones. Make the first stab cuts outside the edges of the higher petals, as shown by the dotted lines in Fig 149c, then proceed to lower the levels of the minor petals. This will make the major ones, which are higher, stand out. All petals will need to roll down towards the flower centre. The edges of the major petals, where they lie on top of the minor ones, can, for the time being, be left with straight sides or, if you prefer, they can be angle-cut now.

Avoid making petals and leaves too shallow, as this will make the design look flat. This is yet another basic rule. If shallow-cut gouges are continually used, as shown in Fig 151a, then the outcome will be little or no contour variation; the carving will remain flat and shallow. If you use gouges with a reasonable depth of cut, much more contour variation will be created. These tools are likely to be in the 5–9 numbering range, and are best worked with a twist as well as a push action. (*See* Fig 151b) It is not uncommon for a design to include elements that need to be rolled over in a convex manner. Examples would be a dipping petal, or a curled leaf. Create the roll effect using the inverted blade of a No. 3 gouge (Fig 151c). Finish off if necessary using the No. 2 skew chisel.

Periodically, take the carving off the board and stand it upright to check the look of the contours. As I recommended in Chapter 11, use an ordinary lamp bulb to cast shadows.

Modelling the Stems (Fig 152)

At the outset, the main stem should be oversize, and so should the stem for the second flower. Once the flowers have been carved, however, the stems will need to be modelled. Firstly, reduce their widths, making sure there is still an even taper. Build in some depth variation. You may need to trim round the main flower seed pod, as well as round the bracts (the two tiny leaves below the flower), as the shape and size of the stem is altered. The ³⁄₁₆in (5mm) No. 7 gouge is sufficiently small to access these parts. Use the small No. 3 gouge inverted, or the skew chisel to round the seed pod. Work with a centre line.

Draw the stems up to a slight ridge along their length; this will reflect light better than if they were simply rounded over. Shaping can be done using the No. 2 skew chisel for the outside bends, but the inside curves are better worked using one of the No. 3 gouges.

Fig 150   Angle-cut petal edges.

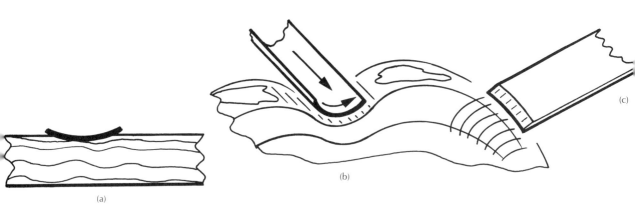

Fig 151   Cutting contours.

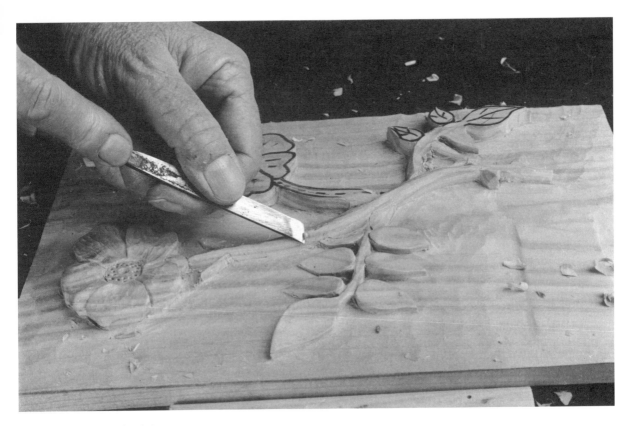

Fig 152   No. 2 skew chisel shaping stem.

For a twiggy, textured look, make small surface cuts on the stems using the No. 6 longpod, and mix in a few veiner cuts.

Leaf Shaping

Those leaves that lie across the run of the grain will be more prone to snapping than those running with the grain, so protect their tips from accidental damage by keeping them close to the background. Leaves that go with the grain can have their tips turned up. If there is any sign of fracture during the final shaping, it is an indication of compression, or stress, during the early 'roughing out' stage. Any resulting breakage may necessitate gaining extra wood, by making a roll-type cut or by dishing the central part of the leaf to increase the surface area.

The division between leaves can be cut using the optional 3/16in (5mm) No. 7 gouge or, if you do not have one of these, the 1/8in (3mm) No. 11. Take care not to dig into the background and make it lower than the remaining part of the carving. One way to ease matters is to 'plane' off some of the excess thickness of wood from the leaves using a No. 3 gouge, and then re-shape their outline. This technique is useful when you come to work on the small leaves which lie close to the main stem.

Strictly speaking, the leaves should have serrated edges, as rose leaves naturally do, but I believe it is a matter of personal opinion whether or not they need to be shown. I decided not to show them, as I was not so concerned with absolutely lifelike representation. In the case of the tiny leaves, the **stipules**, at the base of the left leaf-stalk, I felt they should be shown, albeit in a minor form, as they neatly covered the joint with the main stem.

Undercutting (Fig 153)

The crisp look of a relief carving is enhanced if it can be made to stand out visually from the background. The usual way to achieve this is to undercut some of the more delicately carved parts, such as the petal edges and the edges of the leaves. This will create shadow areas. In olden times, when relief-carved decoration on furniture was popular, craftsmen went as far as to add stain to these undercut parts to increase the shadow effect even more. You may have noticed how, on old furniture, parts of the decoration seem to be grimy. It is very probable that underneath the old wax polish there is some form of dark wood stain. These days, the use of stain is usually omitted, and undercutting alone is carried out.

Undercutting simply consists of making an angled downward cut, followed by a slicing cut, to take out a chip of waste wood. For practical purposes, I tend to do this at the same time as removing the last of the extra background wood – the depth between the dotted line and the true depth line. Any extra deep cuts can then be removed. While the downward cut

Fig 153   Undercutting, steps 1 and 2 shown in bold.

(number 1 in Fig 153) has to be made using a gouge to suit the shape of the edge, the slicing cut (shown as number 2) is best made using a No. 3 gouge.

Background is usually ripple-cut, again using the sweep of a No. 3 gouge. This means that both the ripple cut and the slicing cut can be done at the same time (*See* Fig 154).

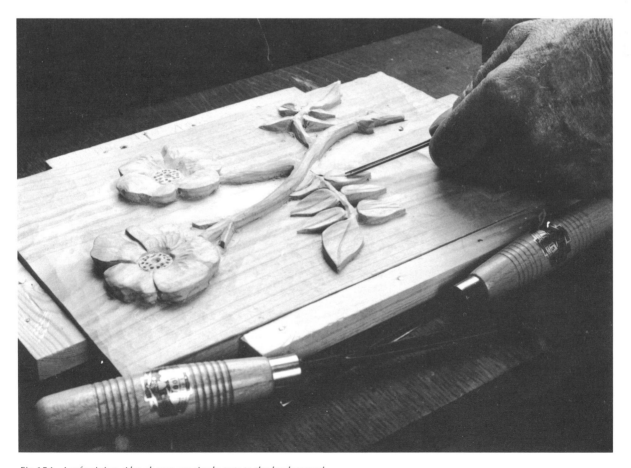

Fig 154   Leaf veining. Also shown are ripple cuts to the background.

A point to note when undercutting is to keep the downward cut at a fairly acute angle; about 60 degrees is ideal. If you drop the angle too much, you might experience difficulty in slicing the chip away cleanly. Take care not to lever the gouge at all, as this could cause a leaf, or whatever part is receiving the treatment, to split.

Just as whether or not to serrate the leaf edges is a matter of personal preference, so is the question of leaf veining. In the case of most leaves, and certainly in that of the rose family, the veins lie within the surface of the upper face; they are only raised on the leaf backs. This means that the veins need to be cut, and then the surrounding wood blended in, so that they do not appear too harsh. The usual way to do this is to use No. 11 veiners of different widths to make the cuts of the long vein and the secondary veins. The edges are then blended back into the surface area of the leaf with slicing or paring cuts made with the tip of the skew chisel, or corner of a No. 3 gouge blade. Clearly, you have a problem if your choice of veining tools is limited, as the veins could end up out of proportion to the size of the leaf. This problem is made worse by the fact that if you want to do sub-veins, as well as the main ones which run the length of the leaves, they will need to be smaller still. For these reasons, it is not at all unusual for carvers to employ a V-tool rather than a veiner. The width of cut can then be adjusted by the amount of downward pressure applied. The No. 41 V-tool with its narrow cut is ideal, better in fact than the No. 39 type, which, because it cuts a 45-degree V channel, can be too wide. The edges of the cuts will still have to be blended back into the leaf surface, though, or the cuts will look harsh and unreal.

Finishing (Fig 155)

During the course of this project, the importance of light reflection has been mentioned more than once. This is more likely to be achieved by retaining cut marks. If you want bright, crisp carvings, go for a tooled finish rather than one produced by excessive sanding. Be sparing with any sanding carried out to remove unwanted marks or fuzzy grain. With regard to the flowers, which are of course a major feature, there are two points worth noting. Firstly, the centres have small depressions. These were made by twisting around the $3/16$in (5mm) No. 7 gouge. (Although the small No. 9 would have done the job as well, it would have made a larger cut.) Secondly, when the centres had been smoothed (by light sanding), each was given a ring of dots – made using a nail with a rounded tip – to simulate the stamen.

The carving was finished with shellac sanding sealer, before being waxed.

Fig 155   Finished Wild Rose.

13

Project Eight – Sunburst

High relief opens up the possibility of creating carvings that have extremes of contour variation. This can impart a considerable measure of visual strength to the work, especially when the fullest use is made of the depth of wood to establish high and low areas of a design.

High relief is better used on solitary items of design. A typical example of its use is on the lion's head, which has always been a popular subject in furniture work. Because of the great amount of depth involved, high relief does not work as well for repetitive designs or complex patterns. One of the reasons for this is the practical way in which areas of deep background can be cleared away for intricate detail to be carved. Low relief is more commonly used where a pattern repeats at regular intervals. If you look at architectural type carving, you will more often than not find that the repeated parts of any design will be in low relief, while the primary elements, such as figures, will be in high contour. These solitary pieces will often be carved in a manner which approaches sculpture.

The manner of working in high relief, is quite different to the way in which the dog rose was fashioned in the previous project. To learn something of these differences, try carving the sun symbol. It will enable you to experience carving to a greater depth than you did in the last project. It should help you to appreciate fully the need for good contour variation, and you should find carving the face both rewarding and satisfying. It will, I hope, give you the confidence to try, on your own, further work on the human form; even as far as carving the likeness of someone you know. As it is imaginary, there is plenty of latitude in this design. If the shape has to be altered because things start to go wrong it will not really matter.

DRAWING THE DESIGN (Figs 157 and 158)

The sun is round – so should the face be. It will be good if, throughout the whole of the drawing of the design, and its subsequent carving, this thought is kept in mind. Try and fix your thoughts on the roundness needed; the design is round in circumference and it is curved in its sectional shape. The wood is 2in (50mm) thick and every scrap of this will be required if the shape is to be full and round. Carrying out this project will help you to gain basic knowledge of how faces, or for that matter heads, need to be designed and carved. It will help you to avoid the all-too-common fault of making the face too flat.

YOU WILL NEED

Wood:
This is a typical occasion when it is best to begin by choosing the wood, and then doing the design. The width of the timber used is going to dictate how big the circumference of the sunburst can be, if all the flames are to be of an equal length. Also, you need to make your choice knowing that the wood has to be of a type that is strong on the cross-grain, with well-bonded cells. If these properties are not considered, there could be problems ahead when the flames are cut, since at least half of them will be on cross-grain.

The wood used for this carving was Lime, measured 14¾in (375mm) long, 10in (255mm) wide, and 2in (50mm) thick, and the grain ran vertically. An alternative choice of timber would have been Sycamore, but there are few other woods which have a comparable degree of cell strength. This does not mean you could not carve the sun symbol in another wood, like Oak for instance. It is simply easier, and safer, to do it in Lime.

Tools:

¼in (6mm) No. 3	¼in (6mm) No. 9
½in (13mm) No. 3 fishtail	½in (13mm) No. 9
¾in (20mm) No. 3	⅜in (10mm) No. 2 skew
¾in (20mm) No. 4	¼in (6mm) No. 41 V-tool
¾in (20mm) No. 5	

Fig 156   Project 8 – Sunburst.

Because the sun is round, you need to think in terms of basing the construction on circles. The method used is, in this respect, similar to that used to depict early religious portraits. The style is known as Byzantine, and utilises a layout of three concentric circles. When you produce other faces, in the future, you can use the same method of proportion, but some 'stretching' of the circles upwards and downwards may be needed if you are to arrive at shapes that are more oval, and more similar to the true shape of the human head.

The design consists of three concentric circles, with their centres located at the mid-point of the face. The radius of the innermost circle is equal to the length of the nose, and it can determine the width of the eyes.

The second circle, with a radius equal to twice the length of the nose, fixes the size of the head. The third and outer circle describes the halo, and can have a radius of three nose lengths.

The width of the wood (10in, or 255mm) dictates the circumference of the halo, so drawing the circles means having first to decide the width of a halo that can possibly be accommodated, then establishing the length of the nose and the size of the head by using the appropriate circles.

Draw two lines to plot the vertical and horizontal mid-points, and mark a circle of 10in (255mm) in diameter, with its centre at the junction of the two lines. This circle is the halo circumference.

From this circle you can judge the width required

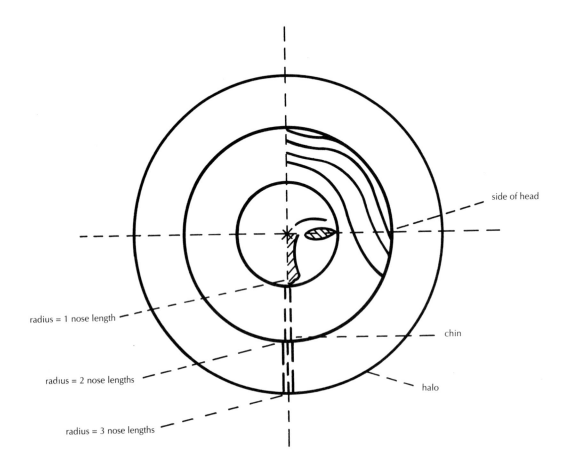

radius = 1 nose length

radius = 2 nose lengths

radius = 3 nose lengths

side of head

chin

halo

Fig 157   Project Eight – design is based on three concentric circles.

for the halo. This will give you the means of plotting the circumference of the head. Using the Byzantine proportions, you know the radius of the second circle is equal to twice the length of the nose. By halving this measurement, the innermost circle can be drawn, and this will determine the position of the nose and the width of the eyes.

FIXING THE FACIAL FEATURES

You will, I am sure, remember from the earlier projects how you can use a mirror image to make matching left-hand and right-hand shapes. Only one half of the nose, eyes and mouth needs to be drawn: the paper is then reversed to give the mirror image. When I put in the features I decided the face looked best

with the eyes just above the horizontal centre line. For future reference, I sketched in where the cheeks would most probably be.

While the face is stylized, and to a great degree the old adage of 'if it looks right, it is right' applies, there is still a need for it to conform to basic design rules. The size of the eyes and the width of the mouth are typical examples. The following are a few guidelines.
• Approximately 4–5 eye widths are equal to the width of the head.
• Eyes should be set about one eye width apart.
• The distance between the tip of the nose and the bottom of the face divides into three. One third is for the upper lip, one third for the chin, and the third, in the middle, for the mouth. But it should be noted that these measurements are only a rough guide. For example, you might wish to elongate the chin.

Fig 158   Project Eight – Sunburst design.

- The mouth is about 1½ times wider than the eyes.
- The cheeks have to be prominent, but they do not stand out as far as the nose
- The nostrils are flared.

EYES

I plotted the eyes 1½in (32mm) wide. They should not be circular; for a 'happy' look I made the bottom lids straighter than the upper ones.

TONGUES OF FLAME

The halo consists of tongues of flame, that can be styled as you wish; I drew index marks using a protractor, and spaced them 30 degrees apart. The shape of the tongues can be drawn onto the wood using a card template later.

TRANSFER THE DESIGN ONTO THE WOOD

This is done in the usual way with carbon paper. It may be necessary to make some alterations once you have the drawing on the wood, so it is a good idea to use graphite coated, erasable carbon paper, so that any unwanted lines can be rubbed out.

CUT THE OUTER CIRCLE

The wood needs to be cut to the size of the halo. You can do this using a coping saw, but it will be easier if you have access to a bandsaw or a jigsaw.

Index Marks

After the outer circle shape has been cut, put the index lines for the flames onto the wood and extend them to the side edge. They will then be visible when the thickness of the halo is reduced. You can use a protractor, or mark them off using a compass.

Depth Lines

Mark in the depth lines, using bold lines, and dotted lines for the thickness of the halo. For the time being, select 1in (25mm) as the depth, marking the dotted

line just a touch more. This will be sufficient to take care of any stray saw cuts you might make when you remove the waste.

REMOVE WASTE WOOD FROM THE HALO (Fig 159)

Hand-saw as much of the waste wood as you can, making sure the cuts do not go as deep as the dotted depth line.

FIXING THE WOOD

Screw the carving to the backing board, taking care that the screws you use are not too long. Screw in to the thickest part. I used No. 10 size screws, which did not penetrate the carving by more than about ½in (10mm).

Depth of Wood to Spare (Fig 160)

Before you cut anything else, have a look at how much depth there is from the tip of the nose to the halo. Within this depth will lie all the contours of the face. There may seem to be little or no spare wood to allow for mistakes, but in fact there will be a small reserve, because you can adjust the thickness of the halo; you could reduce it to about ½in (say 10mm) if you had to, but this would make the flames that much thinner when you came to carve them.

ROUGHING OUT (Fig 161)

As a matter of course, I used the V-tool to incise around the eyes, nose and mouth. Remember that these features will be reduced in depth and their disposition will alter once the roughing out starts and some of the bulk of the wood is removed. For reference, the high areas – the nose, chin, and cheeks – were marked.

In low relief, creating the rough form is a matter of removing the background and leaving the design in block form for contour shaping during the modelling stage. Because high-relief wood is much thicker, it is not practical to work it in the same manner. If you try to do so, you may not make the best use of the depth of the wood; time will probably be spent hacking

Fig 159   Hand-saw waste in blocks.

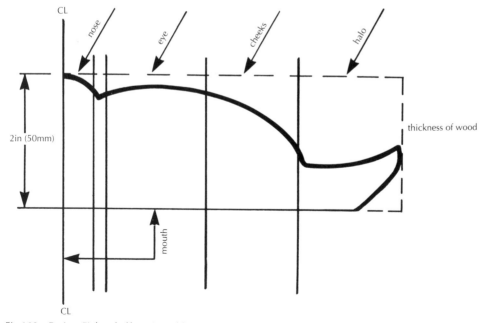

Fig 160   Project Eight – half section of face.

Fig 161   Add contour detail before starting to rough out the shape.

away at it, with the result that the timber ends up thinner than the original plan, and the carving becomes flatter, with less emphasis placed on the contour shaping.

Overcome these problems by first creating the main contours, and then refining the design. In this project, this means creating a curve right across the face *in all directions*. The curves will run from the nose, through the cheeks to the edge of the face and, in the same way, from the brow of the head through to the chin. The curves may only be slight, but they will act as guides for later. They will help to fix in your mind the need to avoid creating a flat surface. As the curving is carried out, you will need to replace the outline detail for the eyes and mouth.

Fig 162, taken when the features had been set in, shows the extent of the curves needed.

It can be a mistake to try and take off too much wood too quickly. If you start cutting with a steep sweep gouge, like a No. 9, you might dig too deep. The contours will be better formed if you take the work slowly, removing only modest amounts with shallow cuts, so use a gouge like the ³/₄in (20mm) No. 5.

SHAPING

Once you have been all the way round using the No. 5 gouge, you need to lower the wood on either side of the nose. Use the ¹/₂in (13mm) No. 9 gouge to keep the groove confined. In other words, the way in which the wood is removed must not interfere with the final height of the cheeks, so, as you make the cuts, keep them from entering the cheek zone. Prevent the gouge from getting stuck by making the groove slightly wider than the width of the tool, or change to the ¹/₄in (6mm) size.

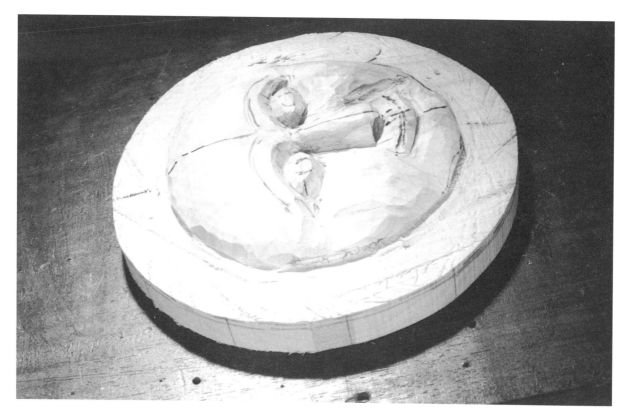

Fig 162   Be sure the front of the face is sufficiently rounded.

MAIN FACIAL CONTOURS

The Mouth

As the facial contours develop, it will be necessary to lower the level of the mouth, and to give it more of a side-to-side curve to make it follow the shape of the face. This will involve some careful stab cutting. Once the outline has been shaped, use the 1/2in (13mm) No. 9 to cut the lower lip. Use the same gouge to trim away at the sides of the mouth, where a shallow groove marks the boundary of the cheeks.

The Upper Lip

This is incorporated into the general shape of the mouth by grading its angle. This angle has to be adjusted as you work on the nostrils. Avoid stab cutting, as the lip has to blend into creases at the sides of the cheeks so a hard line is not wanted.

TIP

The development of the main features needs to be carried out progressively, so that they all advance equally.

The Eyes

The eyes' treatment is similar to that used for the mouth; they have to follow the lateral curve of the head. Create this curve when the depth of the bridge of the nose is being formed, then re-set their outline by stab cutting. For the time being they can be left in block form. Final shaping will take place when the curve of the face is complete.

The Eyebrows

Leave wood for shaping the eyebrows when you work on the forehead.

The Bridge of the Nose

Locate the bridge of the nose at the point which lines up with the upper half of the eyes. Use the ½in (13mm) No. 9 to cut across the top of the bridge to blend it into the forehead without any sharp or hard looking join.

Shape the Nose

Shape the top edge of the nose using one of the shallow-cut gouges upside-down. Blend the sides of the nose into the low area adjoining the cheeks using the No. 11 veiner or the small No. 9 gouge. Cut the nostril cavities using the ¼in (6mm) No. 9.

STAND BACK AND LOOK

When you have worked on the facial features for a little while, stop, stand the work upright, then take a good look. When the carving is not flat on the bench you have a better chance of assessing the progression of the contour shaping. Stand back to give yourself an overall view. You may see small areas that require attention, and that have so far gone unnoticed. For example, I found that the top edge of the sun's face needed to be brought in a fraction, and that some slight adjustment was needed to give more definition to the chin.

MORE WORK ON THE EYES (Figs 163–166)

When I was looking at my work it occurred to me that because the sun is bright, perhaps the eyes should be screwed up a little, rather than being fully open. This meant bringing both eyebrows down into creases at the sides of the eyes. Being a stylization, these creases could be rather exaggerated. The upper lid also needed to be dropped to a fraction above the halfway line.

Fig 163   Cut the eyelid to the depth of the eyeball . . .

Fig 164   ... follow with a slicing cut.

Carving the eyes is not as difficult as it might first seem. The whole of the eye has first to be shaped using the inside sweeps of the No. 4 and No. 3 gouges. I also found the ¹/₂in (13mm) No. 3 fishtail useful. Use them upside down to make the rounded shape of the eyeball. At this stage, as well as later, the skew chisel is useful for getting into the corners.

Once this has been done, the lower lid can be set in. Cut the outline of the lid with light stab cuts. Use the ³/₄in (20mm) No. 3 gouge, as only a slight shape is required. Trim the waste off using the No. 3 fishtail. It is essential that both stab and trimming cuts meet cleanly. Listen for a crunching sound as you cut; it is a sure sign that you are making the cuts properly and that the tools are really sharp.

The upper lid is cut in a similar way, but the edge needs more of a curve, so cut using the ³/₄in (20mm) No. 4, if not the No. 5.

When finished, the edge of the lower lid can incline up to the eyeball. In the case of the upper lid, however, the edge needs to be undercut. This will introduce a line of shadow, which gives the impression of eyelashes.

The eyeball will usually protrude too much once the lids have been modelled, so it will need to be refined in size and shape. You can do some of the work at the front of the eye by cutting with an inverted ¹/₄in (6mm) No. 3 gouge, but better results will be achieved by making rolling cuts with the skew chisel. Do this by keeping the bevel rubbing against the wood all the time you are cutting. This will prevent the point from digging in.

The eyeball should look as if it is a round ball, filling the oval surround of the eye socket.

I left the eyes 'blind', which I thought suited the design better than giving them an iris and a pupil each.

Clean up any rough-cut parts as you go. Finish the eyes by working sanding paper into the corners.

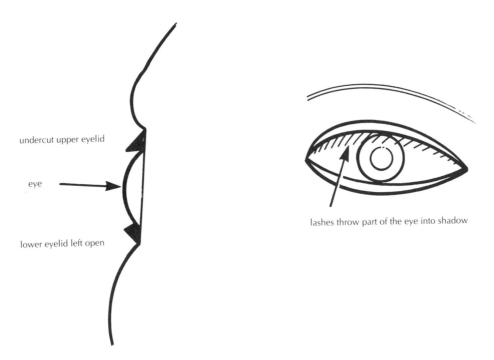

undercut upper eyelid

eye →

lower eyelid left open

lashes throw part of the eye into shadow

Fig 165   As there are no eye lashes you have to undercut the upper lid for shadow.

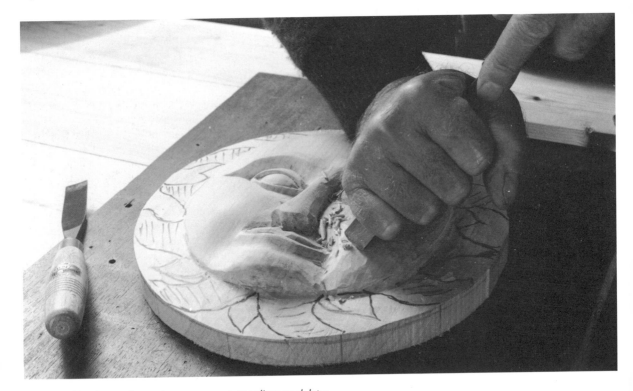

Fig 166   Cleaning up the carving as you go saves tedious work later.

WHERE THE FACE MEETS THE HALO

Where face and halo meet, use the ¼in (6mm) No. 9 gouge to remove waste wood. This tool will leave a rounded cut – easier to clean up when sanding than the harder V-cut. Also the softer shape looks better; you do not want a hard-line division between these two elements of the design. Make certain any lurking saw cuts are removed.

You may need to allow some slight undercutting where the chin and halo meet. This will make the chin more prominent.

SHAPING THE FLAMES (Fig 167)

With the halo smoothed down to an even surface, mark once more the index points from the lines on the halo edge. Then, using a card template cut to the shape you have chosen, draw in the flames. Draw a

mark on the template so that it can be located with the index marks. The shape of the flames may have to be adjusted in places, as shown by comparing those marked below the chin in Fig 163 and in the final picture. Round the points of the flames to avoid them accidentally breaking.

The flames are sawn to shape. Use a coping saw, or a bandsaw with a contour blade. To avoid saw cuts damaging the edge of the face, mark in a safety line just outside its circumference, and only cut to this line. Finish the spaces between each flame by trimming lightly with the ½in (13mm) No. 9. Work the wood from both sides to prevent splitting.

Initially, I left the bottom three flames uncut. This gave me a fixing point whilst the remainder were being shaped. Later, with suitable padding, the finished part of the halo could be clamped whilst the last three segments were carved.

Contour shape the flames, using the ¾in (20mm) No. 5 gouge, applying the twisting action shown in

Fig 167   Shaping the flames of the halo. Note the uncut part for vice gripping.

Fig 151. Finish off by smoothing with abrasive paper wrapped around a sanding stick of the approximate thickness of a broom handle. Concentrate on shaping the fronts. Use a smaller sanding stick to work the curves in between each flame.

FEATHER-EDGING (Fig 168)

Feather-edging is the illusory way of making something seem slimmer than it really is. You will recall it was used on the dolphin in Project 3, when the fins were being shaped.

Once the upper surface of the flames has been shaped, the back of each flame can be angle-cut using a tenon saw or a coping saw. If you use a tenon saw make sure that the blade is really sharp (with a coping saw fit a new blade), as it is vital that the wood is not stressed at all while being cut; it could lead to the flame ends breaking. Finish the shape from behind using coarse abrasive. Its use is less likely to damage the tips than rasp or gouge. A small drum sander on a flex-drive shaft will do the work very well. Be sure to use some form of cushion for protection when you have the carving face-down on the bench.

While working on the back, I fitted a recessed key-plate for use when hanging the sun symbol.

FINISHING TREATMENT (Fig 169)

The way in which the carving is finished is a matter of personal preference. You may wish to leave the natural colour of the wood and simply treat it with sealer and wax, or there is the popular option of using gilt varnish or gilding cream. Another possibility is to use

Fig 168   Using a tenon saw to 'feather' the backs of the flames.

a subtle colour wash, and then to sprinkle on some gilt powder to look like gold dust. Whatever choice you make, try it out first on scrap wood.

Fig 169   The finished Sunburst.

14

Project Nine – Mirror Frame

Mirrors are not difficult to produce. They are practical, as well as making useful gifts. Even a small reflection will give an extra dimension to relief work, by adding further depth to its overall appearance.

The range of designs is vast. Once you start to think of making mirrors, you will find you can easily pick up ideas from book illustrations, or from greeting cards; then you can make sketches, using coloured card to represent the mirror glass.

In this project the mirror represents a pool of water. It is surrounded by willows and perched on one of the branches is a kingfisher, gazing hopefully into the water. To avoid the frame seeming to be top-heavy,

three small cut-outs were added, in addition to the main opening, with the mirror extending behind them.

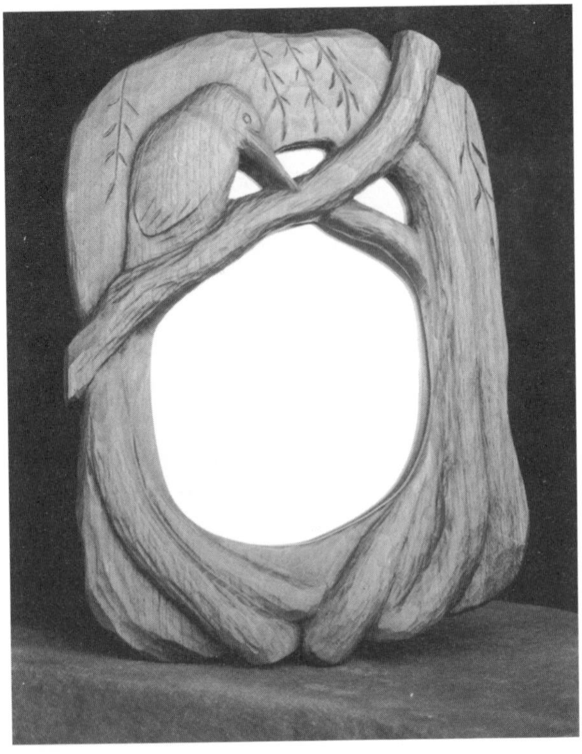

CHOICE OF WOOD (Fig 171)

If you keep the mirror frame's width to not more than 10in (250mm), you can work with wood from sawn boards; using woods like Lime, Sycamore, Cherry, Chestnut or Oak, which are all generally available in widths to suit. There will then be no need to glue narrow pieces together.

As mentioned when we first looked at relief work, have the tips of the annual rings pointing upwards. Alternatively, choose quarter-sawn timber, cut from the widest part of the tree. The more vertical position of the annual rings will give greater stability and the linear figuring will not detract from the look of the carving.

If you are not going to be able to start work on the frame as soon as the wood has been planed for thickness, then keep it in clamps, as shown in Fig 172, to prevent warping.

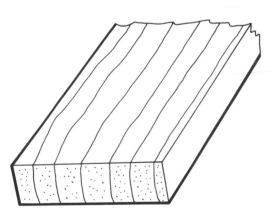

Fig 170   Project Nine – Mirror Frame.

Fig 171   Quarter-sawn timber.

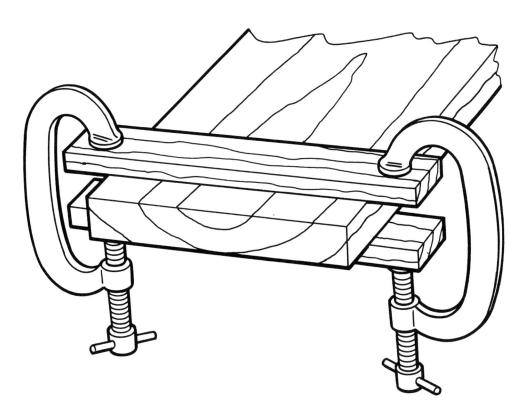

Fig 172   Clamp both ends to prevent warping.

My piece of Sweet Chestnut measured 14in long, 10¼in wide and 1¼in thick – 355mm × 260mm × 32mm.

Chestnut Can Be Fumed

I chose to use Sweet Chestnut, because it is an easy wood to carve and, when finished and polished, it is attractive to look at. As one of the two main timbers that contain tannic acid – the other being Oak – the colour can be changed to a darker shade by the action of ammonia. This process, very popular years back, is known as 'fuming' and we shall be looking at how it is done later in this chapter.

USING THE DESIGN (Figs 173–176)

Fig 173 shows the overall design, seen from the front. Note that it includes, shown by a broken line, the

---

YOU WILL NEED

The carving tools I used were taken from those in the recommended list. They included:

³⁄₈in (10mm) No. 2 skew chisel	½in (13mm) No. 7
	¼in (6mm) No. 9
¼in (6mm) No. 3,	½in (13mm) No. 9
¾in (20mm) No. 4	⅛in (3mm) No. 11,
³⁄₁₆in (5mm) No. 7	¼in (6mm) No. 41 V-tool

In addition, you will need to use a **drill** with a **½in (13mm) flat bit**, and also a smaller **twist bit** of about ³⁄₁₆in **(5mm)** diameter for making holes prior to sawing the voids. For cutting the mirror voids themselves, you will need a **coping saw**, and, for the large opening, a **jigsaw**.

To recess the back of the frame, where the mirror fits, you need a **router** with a straight fluted cutter. If a router is not used, the rebate can be cut using a **chisel**.

Do not be put off, though, if you have not got these tools. They are commonly used in woodwork and by making a few enquiries locally you should find a friendly hobbyist who will help with the cutting.

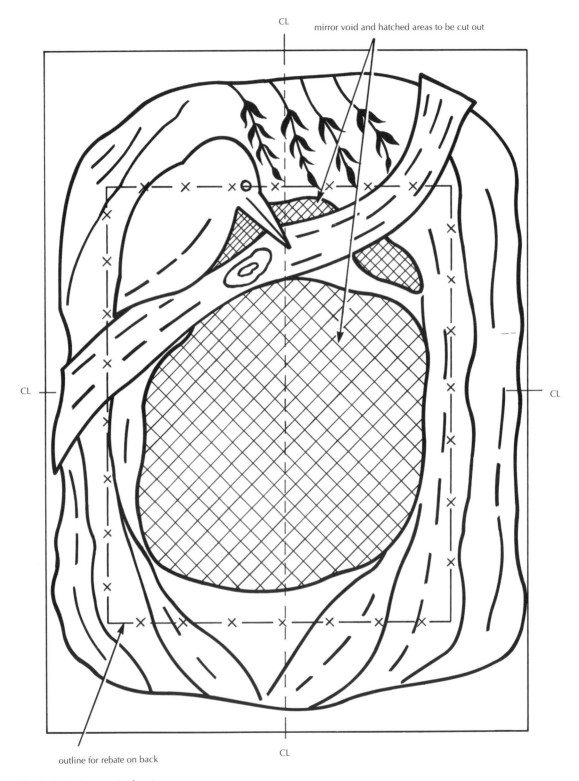

CL

mirror void and hatched areas to be cut out

CL

CL

CL

outline for rebate on back

Fig 173   Project Nine – main drawing.

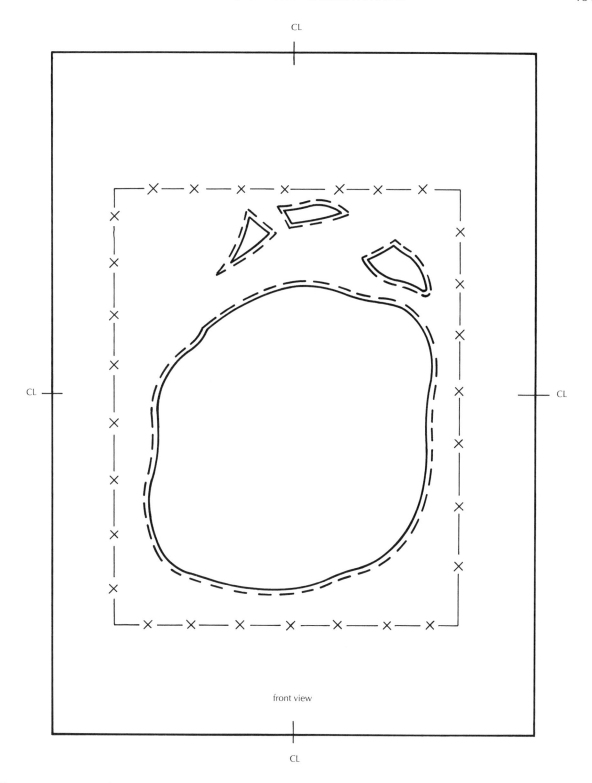

CL

CL

CL

CL

front view

Fig 174   Project Nine – front view of cut-outs.

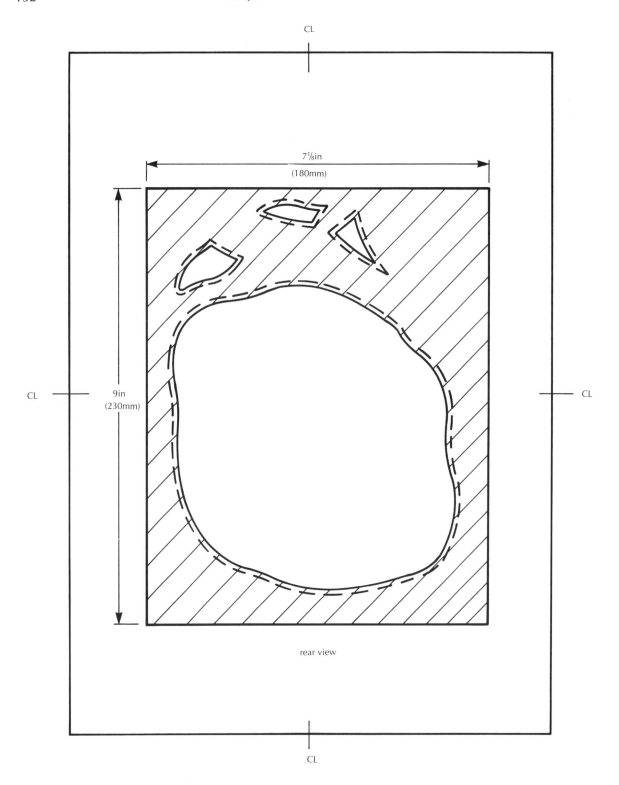

CL

7⅛in
(180mm)

9in
(230mm)

CL

CL

rear view

CL

Fig 175   Project Nine – rear view of the mirror rebate and cut-outs.

position of the mirror recess. When you are carving, it will be vital to know where this lies, as it marks the boundary between thick and thin wood.

Fig 174 shows the front view of the mirror cut-outs. Also shown (as an –x–) is the mirror recess *at the rear of the carving*.

Fig 175 shows the rear view. The bold line is the extent of the mirror recess.

Precise alignment of the front and rear drawings is important. You will see that each has locating marks on both the vertical and horizontal axes.

First of all you will need to have corresponding lines drawn on the front and back of the wood. Then, using scissors or a craft knife, snip 'V'-cuts where the locating marks occur on each drawing (Fig 176).

Figs 174 and 175 show the cut-outs having both a full line and broken lines. The broken lines relate to the voids marked in the main drawing, while the full lines are cutting guides for when you saw out the voids. Note that the openings either side of the beak will be enlarged later, when the beak itself is carved.

TIP

Leave sufficient space between the rim of the main voids and the edges of the mirror, so that the reflection of the edges cannot be seen.

Don't worry if the area of the main cut-out looks a little on the small side when drawn on the wood; it will look larger once the mirror glass is fitted.

• Apply the main drawing (Fig 173) to the face of the wood.

• Overdraw the cut-outs, using Fig 174.

• Use the rear drawing Fig 175 for the back.

• CHECK THAT Figs 174 and 175 line up with each other.

• When the entire design has been copied, go over the lines, using a felt-tipped pen, to make them easy to see.

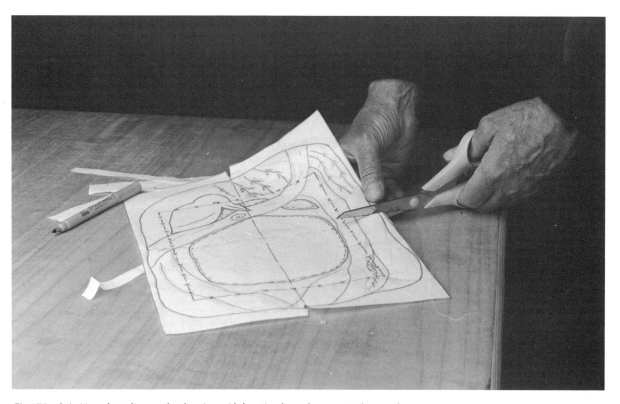

Fig 176   Snip V marks to line up the drawing with locating lines drawn onto the wood.

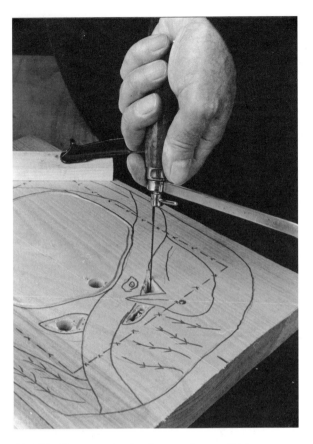

Fig 177 Open up cut-outs using a coping saw. (Note V-lines on cut-outs.)

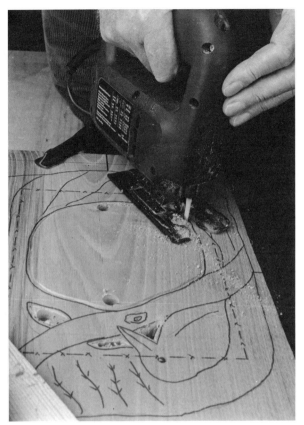

Fig 178 Cutting the main void using a jigsaw.

MAKING THE CUT-OUTS (Figs 177 and 178)

Working on the face of the carving, incise using the V-tool on or just inside the unbroken lines marking the voids. These will be saw-cut. Make certain you keep within the dotted lines – this will avoid taking off too much wood and regretting it later!

Pilot holes need to be drilled, to provide entry for either the jigsaw or the coping saw. The main mirror cut-out can be drilled using the flat bit if the jigsaw is to be used. Smaller-sized holes may be needed for the three minor voids, if cut using a coping saw. Place these in the middle of each space.

Cut on the V-line for the main mirror. In the case of the minor voids do not cut right up to the beak or up to the diagonal branch, for the time being. Leave these holes until the carving is being set in. Do not

discard the wood from the main cut-out, as it will be needed when routing the rebate.

CUTTING THE REBATE (Figs 179 and 180)

Turn the wood over and, on the back, V-tool just *inside* the rebate line where the mirror is to go. Do all the initial cutting to this V-line, then trim to the design line afterwards.

It is best if the rebate is cut using a router, as the depth can be accurately gauged. As mentioned earlier, if you do not own one yourself, make a few local enquiries, as there is bound to be a keen woodworker in your neighbourhood who will give you a hand. Alternatively, try the woodwork department at your local school. If all else fails, however, the rebate can still be cut using a chisel for the vertical sides and a gouge to take out the waste.

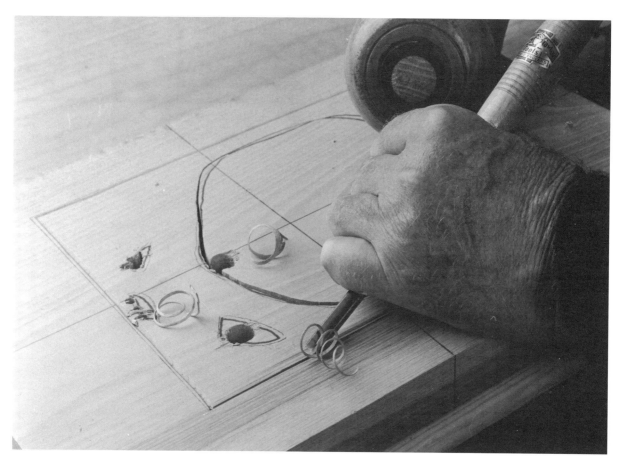

Fig 179   V-tool the rebate outline.

When cutting the depth, it is preferable to work in metric measurement. A depth of 10mm (³⁄₈in) is required. This will accommodate the mirror glass and a backing board, each with a 4mm thickness, and leave 2mm spare to take up any subsequent wood distortion. Cut to a depth of 10mm.

Replace the piece you cut for the main mirror opening, so that the router has a level surface, then cut the rebate up to the V-tooled line.

When the rebate has been taken down to the required depth, trim the edges to the final size. For the long runs it is best to use a standard, bevel-edge chisel of about 1in (25mm) wide, with the flat of the blade facing the measured line. For cleaning out the corners, use the No. 2 skew, as its shape will allow you to work the tip right into the corner. Skew chisels, incidentally, are also known as corner chisels.

The mirror needs a good-sized rebated ledge to sit on, which means there has to be sufficient overlap from the edge of the mirror to the sides of the main opening. If the ledge is too narrow at any point, the edge of the mirror's glass will be visible when seen from the front. With care, however, it is possible to extend the opening to the full size and shape shown in the drawings. Working with the frame face up, do this by cutting carefully with the ¹⁄₄in (6mm) No. 3 gouge, taking shallow slicing cuts. Or, if preferred, use a medium-cut wood rasp. Keep some waviness to the shape; it will look better than when symmetrical.

At this stage you can increase the size of the minor openings, still leaving spare wood around the bird's beak.

Fig 180   Routing the mirror recess.

HOLDING THE CARVING

Up to this point it was possible to use G-clamps to hold the work in place. From now on, throughout all the carving sequence, I prefer to hold the wood so that it can be easily turned around, or lifted up for viewing. However, instead of pinning the battens on the outside to a backing board, as I did in the earlier relief carving, I fitted two rectangular pieces of 10mm-thick ply into the mirror recess, and pinned them to my bench-held mounting board. This meant the outer edge of the mirror frame could be shaped without any holding difficulty.

Depth Line

With this method of holding, it is possible to see the depth of the wood where the rebate is. It does no harm at all, however, to mark a corresponding line on the outside of the wood; in fact, it can be a positive advantage to know exactly where the rebate is when

carving, and to know that there is sufficient depth of wood. Otherwise there is the possibility of cutting through the walls of the rebate as you shape the branches. Give yourself wood to spare by marking the depth line higher than the rebate depth.

INCISE THE OUTLINE

Use the V-tool to incise all the design outline, cutting, as usual, into the wood which will become waste.

SHAPING THE FRAME

Before you begin to create the contours, shape the outer edge. Cut using a bandsaw, a jigsaw, or even a coping saw. The edges of some of the branches can be allowed to extend beyond the main perimeter shape. This will bring more realism to the look of your work.

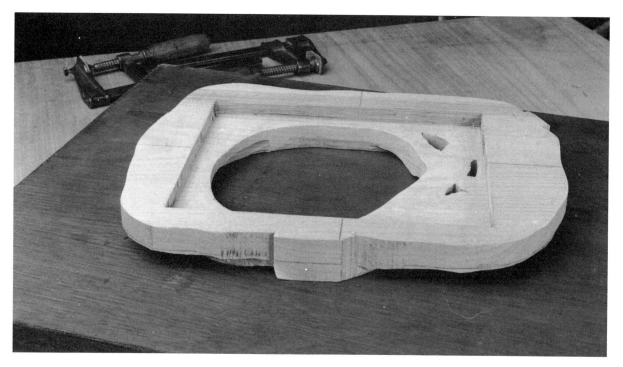

Fig 181   Mirror recess.

HIGHS AND LOWS

The next stage is to determine which parts of the design are high contour areas, and which are the low ones. You can mark them with coloured chalk.

The highest part is represented by the diagonal branch supporting the kingfisher. The lowest parts are the surrounds at the top and the bottom of the mirror opening. Next lowest is the small diagonal branch which lies under the right-hand minor void, as well as the area containing the willow leaves. Remember that the 'low' and 'lowest' parts have to be reconciled with the wood required for the mirror rebate.

CONTOUR SHAPING (Fig 182)

When you look at the design on the wood it can be a problem knowing where to begin carving. I started by lowering the small bridging branch which lies at the top right of the mirror. (The reason for choosing this spot was that it is in the rebated part of the design. By fixing its depth I then had a yardstick with which to judge other low-lying parts.) I then moved on to low-

ering the wood surrounding the bird's head and back. I needed to watch the rebate in the top left corner, which falls in this area. This was followed by reducing the wood around the main diagonal branch.

Next, the thickness of the bird itself was reduced slightly.

I kept a steep angle cut between the bottom of the body and the branch the bird sits on. I did not want the kingfisher to look as if it were slipping off its perch!

Where branches overlap, do not make the division between them too defined at the beginning. If you stab-cut downwards using a chisel or shallow gouge, you are likely to leave marks in the wood. These can remain right through to the completion of the work and cause you problems when you come to the finishing stage. It is better to clear the bulk of the surplus wood using a rounded gouge, like the No. 9, or even by using the No. 11 veiner; in either case the curved shape of the cut will take off most of the waste yet still leave a tiny amount of spare wood along the edge of each branch. The remainder can be tidied up later with light cuts made using a shallow gouge or a chisel without leaving stab marks. Another place to

Fig 182   Forming the background level. Also shown is part of the holding struts.

return curve of the top of the branch. This gives the impression that it is passing *behind* the branch, as the body of the bird starts to turn when it spies something in the water. Consequently, the tail, the rear part of the bird's body, and the branch all need to be carved as one entity, at the same time, and not as separate and specific elements carved individually.

The opening of the mirror has to be angled in the same way as, in architecture, thick walls are made to slope into a window to reveal more light. This gives the impression that the mirror space is larger than it really is. It also helps to avoid the appearance of heavy looking edges. Slope the wood by cutting with the ³/₄in (20mm) No. 4 or No. 3 gouge for the sides and the bottom, and with the ¹/₂in (13mm) No. 7 for the bends, as well as in the minor gaps. By changing over from the flatter and broader shape, there will be less of a chance that the blade will jam as it cuts the curves.

SHAPING THE BRANCHES

The branches will need to have centre lines, so their shape will be balanced. They should not be too tapered. When you shape up to the centre line, do it by making short, cutting strokes. These will give a random-type cut finish, and a more realistic look than a totally smooth surface. Shape where you can, using one of the shallow-cut gouges inverted – the ³/₄in (20mm) No. 4 works well. For shaping the curved parts, use the No. 2 skew chisel.

CROSSING BRANCHES

When you reach the point where one branch crosses another, it is not necessary to carve each to its full depth. In fact, only half the thickness of each will be required for the junction to look right.

CARVING THE KINGFISHER

There should be no problem when you come to carving the kingfisher, but you will find it best to think through the various stages before cutting any wood.

use the rounded tools is at junction points, as the softer line can look better; too hard a line may look unnatural.

Like most other types of carving, it is best to work over the entire piece, rather than confining one's attention for too long a time to one specific area. By working the whole piece through the various stages, you will keep more of an even balance to all the elements of the design. Concentrate for too long in one spot, and it may well not blend in as well with the area around it. For example, do not spend too much time trying to shape up the bird before the surrounding wood has received attention; if you concentrate on the bird for too long, you could find that its general appearance looks less like the rest of the work. Take the tail as an example: it is short and stubby, and does not really need to be set in as a primary feature. In fact, the tail looks best when it blends into the

TIPS

1 It is essential that the bird looks alert. Try and get the line of sight through the tip of the beak correct.
2 The beak is dagger-like in shape. Do not make it too slim.
3 Shape the beak using the No. 2 skew chisel.
4 Where the upper and the lower mandibles meet, create a ridge along the length of the beak. This will make a highlight. Incise it, using the V-tool, along its length to give further emphasis.
5 A kingfisher needs to have a hunched-up look, with the head drawn back into the body; keep the shoulder line full.
6 As you model the bird, stand the frame on end periodically to assess its shape. Because of the perspective needed if the bird is to seem to be looking into the water, you may find it necessary to make slight adjustments to the shape of the head, and some foreshortening may be needed. Check this when the frame is upright; you will not be able to see what is required to improve the perspective with the carving lying on the bench.

7 Whatever else happens when you set about carving the bird, do be sure it sits squarely on the branch, and does not appear to be sliding backwards.
8 The eye and the brow of the head are inter-linked. Even when shown in relief, a bird has to be able to see the tip of its beak, and it can only do this if the curve of the brow is right. Make certain the eye is correctly placed.

CARVING THE HEAD, BEAK AND EYE

I found it best to carry out much of the final shaping of the head and beak using No. 2 skew chisel, making tiny slicing cuts. This requires the bevel to be kept in contact with the wood as a curve develops by constantly adjusting the angle of the blade to the wood. If done correctly, rolling cuts will be made, and the convex curves will be easily formed. Naturally, wher-

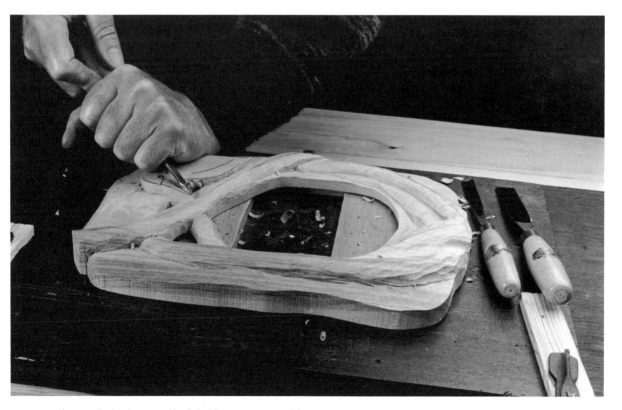

Fig 183 Shaping the beak. Parts of both holding struts are visible.

ever possible, they should be carried out with the lie of the grain. If you are at all doubtful of your ability to make cuts like this, then use the curve of the inside sweep of the small No. 3 gouge.

TEXTURE CUTTING (Fig 184)

With much of the carving consisting of exposed end-grain, which is difficult to smooth, other than by cutting with a razor-sharp blade, there is much merit in opting for a textured finish.

Using the $^3/_{16}$in (5mm) No. 7 gouge, shown in the original list as an optional tool or, alternatively, the $^1/_4$in (6mm) No. 6 longpod, the surface of the boughs can be given striation to simulate bark.

The same tools can be used to provide feathering to the head and breast of the kingfisher, using very short length cuts to create a dappled look.

The lines of the flight feathers were reproduced by grooving parts of the wings using the V-tool. Only a few cuts were needed.

The willow leaves would have been unsuitable if shaped in raised relief. The reason for this is that their tips, on short grain, would have been too vulnerable, and breakages would have been unavoidable. Instead, they were incised into the wood using the V-tool, as shown in the picture.

FUMING

After a light sanding to remove wisps of fibres, the carving could have been sealed and waxed in the usual way, but, since Chestnut wood is light in colour, I felt it would benefit by being darkened. Instead of using a wood dye, I opted to use the older method of fuming.

Fig 184   Cutting willow leaves using the V-tool.

A hundred years or so ago, fuming was regularly practised as a means of darkening, without using stain, either Oak or Chestnut. Its use is less popular these days, maybe because people are unaware how easy it is to carry out.

Fuming works because of the reaction to ammonia vapour of the tannic acid found in Oak or Chestnut. You cannot produce the effect on most other woods, as they do not possess tannin. Carry out the procedure out of doors.

Step 1 **Read the instructions** on the bottle of ammonia before you begin.

Step 2 Pour about half a cup of ordinary household ammonia into a shallow dish.

Step 3 Place it near the wood you wish to fume, in a reasonably airtight container. Use a large plastic bag made into a wigwam with the help of garden canes, or an upside-down dustbin. A plastic garden cloche works well for small carvings, and if you can see what is going on inside so much the better, as you will then know when to stop the process – otherwise you have to guess the time needed.

Step 4 Leave the carving and the ammonia inside for about 20–30 minutes, by which time there should be a noticeable colour change to the wood. The longer you leave it exposed to the ammonia, the darker the wood will get.

Step 5 When you think the carving has had long enough, take it out and run cold water over it to neutralize any ammonia on the wood. If you do not do this the carving will keep on 'cooking' and get darker.

SAFETY TIP

Ammonia vapour will irritate your eyes – that is why this procedure is best done outside, not in the kitchen!

MIRROR GLASS AND BACKING

You will find that mirror glass is quite cheap to buy. It is sold by good old-fashioned glaziers or hardware shops, and there should be no difficulty in getting it cut to the size you need.

For the backing use plywood or MDF board.

Both the mirror and the backing need to have a loose fit in the recessed part of the frame. Leave a gap of about $1/8$in (2–3mm) so that the wood can distort without cracking the mirror. You can buy mirror clips to hold the glass and the backing in place, but they always seem quite large for the job, so for this project I bought some plastic cleats from a picture framer, which worked well and looked much neater.

For hanging the mirror, use picture wire and screw eyes, or, as I did, a key-plate.

15

Project Ten –
Blackbird, Branches and Leaves

In this final project, many of the threads of technique explored in the earlier work have been drawn together. New ground is also covered. To avoid repetition, I have kept my explanations concise where the basic work is similar to that carried out previously. I have concentrated mainly on the principal aspects of producing a two-part carving, to show how to use a composition of ideas, rather than a subject mounted on a simple plinth. My choice for this project was a blackbird perched upon leaves and branches.

PERCEPTION

This project involves carving a bird from one piece of wood, then mounting it onto a carving of branches and leaves to form the base. Where the two meet there is a 'cushion' of leaves. This overcomes the problem of having to carve the bird's thin legs. To give a feeling of movement, the bird's head is turned and tilted.

Working drawings for the bird are shown, but I have only included a rough sketch of the base to encourage individual expression.

Fig 185 Project Ten concept.

Wood:
Since it is becoming more difficult to obtain large section timber, carvers are having to face the prospect of either laminating wood to make one larger block, or using smaller pieces of timber for component parts of a design, such as this bird and base, joining them together later. This method has in fact been used for very many years. Much of Grinling Gibbons's work was produced using this 'build-up' technique. Apart from being more economical, this process has the advantage that the wood will be more stable and less prone to splitting than a large block would be, as there is less shrinkage.

The wood I used was Elm, although any other hardwood, such as Lime, Chestnut or Sycamore could have been used. Before being cut to its final size, the wood for the bird measured 9in (230mm) in length, 4½in (115mm) deep, and 4in (100mm) wide. Later, another piece of Elm was chosen for the base. It contained a band of a lighter colour. Initially, it measured 14in (355mm) long, 5in (130mm) deep, and 4½in (115mm) wide.

Tools:
The tools used were much the same as in the foregoing projects, and do not, I feel, merit listing in full once more. For body shaping, the No. 5 and No. 7 gouges were used most, along with the shallow-cutting Nos. 3, 4 and 5. For the base, the No. 9 gouges, both ¼in (6mm) and the larger one, proved useful, especially when widening out the drilled hole. My favourite, the ¼in (6mm) No. 6 longpod, was used for leaf modelling.

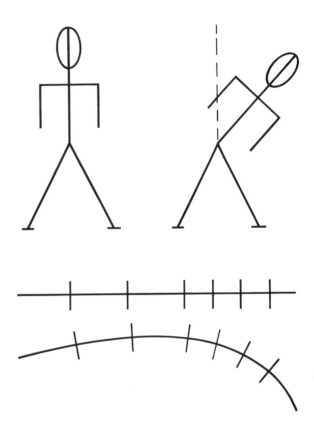

Fig 186   *The effect of changing axis.*

DRAWINGS (Fig 187)

To depict a sense of alertness, you need to think in terms of giving the head a tilt, or to turn it off-centre. This means there has to be an alteration to the axis.

In this project, turning the head gives it a new horizontal axis (or centre line). Likewise, the tilt of the head means there must also be some re-positioning of the vertical axis. It is important to remember that these changes have taken place when you come to strike off points for positioning the eyes, or to check the curve of the head or the angle of the beak.

It is worth making a sketch showing how the head tilts in the vertical plane. For plotting the plan view, I used separate card templates for both the body and head.

When you come to cut the *profile* shape, it is vital

CHANGE OF AXIS (Fig 186)

Let us consider what happens when part of a design requires a change of axis. Take the vertical axis first: a standing form has an imaginary line running vertically through its centre. This is the axis. When part of the form changes position, the corresponding part of the axis moves in sympathy. The point to note is that the parts of the form, when taking up their new positions, do so with just the same angles to the new axis as they had with the old. So, the head and shoulders of the stick-man keep their respective places, as the body tilts with shoulders remaining at right-angles to the new axis line.

The same thing happens horizontally. As the axis takes up a new position, lines crossing it have to reform *just as they did with the vertical axis; they must do this at right-angles to the axis line.*

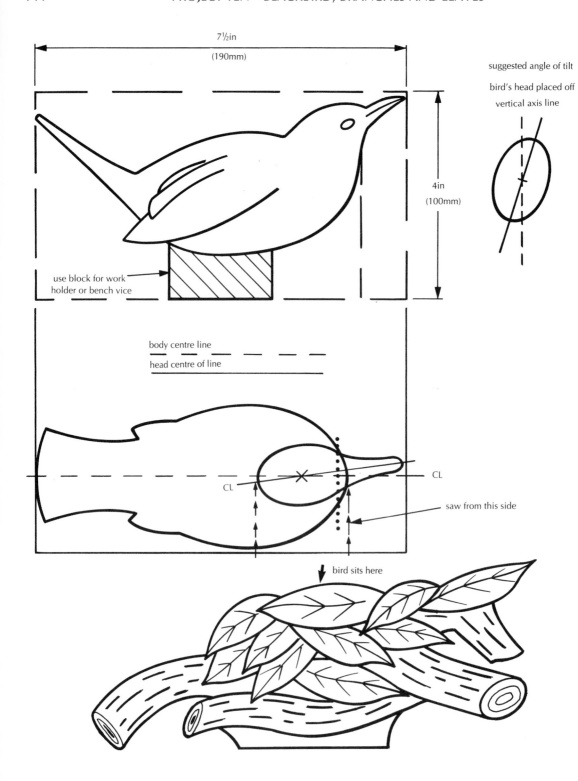

7½in
(190mm)

suggested angle of tilt

bird's head placed off
vertical axis line

4in
(100mm)

use block for work
holder or bench vice

body centre line

head centre of line

CL

CL

saw from this side

bird sits here

Fig 187   Project Ten – profile and plan views.

to know from which side of the block this should be done. On the plan view, this is shown by arrows. You will see that I have also included a dotted line to show what would happen if the front of the head were to be cut from the wrong side.

CONSTRUCTION

Stage 1 – Imprint Profile Drawing

If you are following my layout, put the profile drawing on the right-hand side of the block used for the bird. Do this in the usual way, using carbon paper. Look carefully at the imprint and make any changes which may better suit the grain pattern to the wood. For example, I altered the beak slightly to match the wood.

Stage 2 – Using the Templates

If you have made templates for the body and head, it is a good idea to pin them to the wood at this stage, and before you do any cutting, just to check how they match up with the profile. You will also be able to make certain you know which will be the side to cut

from – as shown by the small arrows on the plan view.

Stage 3 – Cut to Profile

V-tool the profile outlines, leaving extra room around both the body and the head for modifications later. Then saw the wood to the V-cut shape.

Stage 4 – Plan View (Fig 188)

Once more, use the templates. Because of the undulations of the profile cut-out, neither will now fit very well, but they will still be sufficiently accurate to act as a reasonable guide. Pin or hold the body template, hand draw and make any modifications needed. You will need to draw in the *body* centre line.

Next, position the template for the head, and set it to the angle needed to turn the head sideways. Note that the centre of the head, shown as 'X' on the plan drawing, has to fall on the body centre line, or the head will be out of alignment.

Once the head template is in the correct position,

Fig 188   Project Ten – first cut the head in block form.

Fig 189   Make sure that there is enough spare wood for the faceplate screws – pack out if necessary.

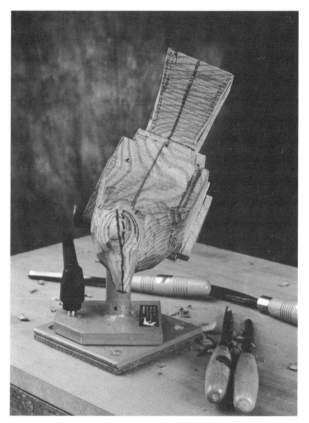

Fig 190   A change of centre line can improve the look. The dotted line is the original. The new line makes better use of annual ring configuration.

draw round it, then use a tenon saw to cut out a rectangular block.

Stage 5 – Body Shaping (Fig 189)

The plan view body outline will need to be cut using a handsaw. It is complicated by the block you have to leave for mounting to the workholder faceplate (assuming a workholder is being used), or for holding in a vice. Unless you are using a small faceplate, the block will need to be wider than the bird's body. I left the block the original width of the wood and trimmed around it for the body shape. I had to make certain that enough wood was left for the screws fixing the wood to the faceplate.

Stage 6 – Tilt of Head (Fig 190)

You will soon reach a point when no more sawing

can be done, and from then on it is a case of using only gouges for waste removal. Start by finalizing the tilt of the head, on the vertical axis, since this is the key to the whole carving. Once the head is blocked out, albeit larger than its final size, the remainder of the bird is relatively easy to produce.

When you start the gouge work the head may appear to be buried in the body. As the sides of the body are reduced, however, and the curve of the back is formed, this will be rectified. Avoid making the neck too long.

At this juncture, the basic shape should start to evolve. You will need to view it by standing back from it a little, so that you can see the general form you are creating.

The feeling of movement can be spoilt if the angle of tilt, or even the turn of the head, is not in sympathy with the grain of the wood.

Note the dotted centre line as well as the unbroken line. The dotted line was the original centre line I planned to use. Can you see how, by passing to one side of the annual rings, their effect would have been spoilt? The continuous line is the one I used, as it gives better balance, with the rings more in keeping with the shape of the head. By making this change, I needed to shift the body's centre line over a little to the right to compensate. Because there was some extra wood left on the sides of the body, though, the new position did not present any problems. This reinforces the point previously made: if you have wood to spare, you can juggle the shape about and make adjustments without difficulty.

Stage 7 – Wings

In many respects, the wings are similar to those of the owl in Project 1. They lie both on the sides of the body as well as on part of the back. Try and avoid re-creating the popular misconception that the wings are only shown on the sides.

The wings were set in using the V-tool. The body has to be narrower below the line of the wings. There should be more definition towards the tips than at the shoulders. Some flight feathers can be cut using the V-tool.

Blend out any excess wood at the base of the neck, to give emphasis to the shoulders, when you do the next stage.

Stage 8 – Body Shaping (Fig 191)

Blackbirds have a habit of puffing out their feathers when perching, which gives the body a fat look. I endeavoured to capture this, and while I was shaping the body I had to be sure not to make it too slim.

As you reduce the body towards the tail, you will encounter a problem you have met before: when you cut where the tail joins into the body, both dip towards each other, so, if you cut down the length of the tail, you will catch the tool in the opposing upward sweep. Avoid this by cutting at right-angles across the wood where the tail meets the body using the $\frac{1}{2}$in (13mm) No. 9. The steep sweep of this gouge will prevent the blade from snagging.

As you carve below the wing line, you will need to saw-cut into the mounting block. Angle the saw to avoid catching the fixing screws. It helps if the length of the screws is marked on the block beforehand.

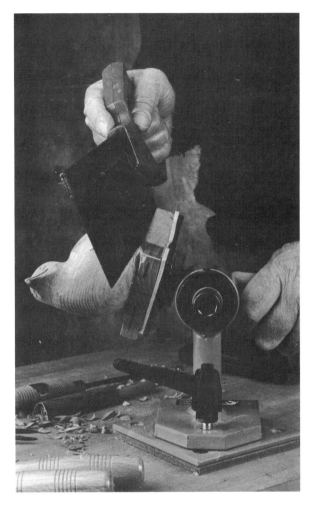

Fig 191   Angle-cut the underside of the bird. The saw needs to miss the fixing screws – mark their positions.

TYPE OF FINISH (Fig 192)

Before the bird is finally separated from its temporary base, you will need to make a choice about the type of finish it should have. Clearly, there will need to be contrast between the ways it and the plinth are treated. What type of contrast, though, is up to you. Which do you 'see' as having the textured surface, the bird, or the branches? Do you think of blackbirds as smooth and branches as rough? Whatever you decide, now is a good time to start thinking about the base. Select the wood you will use, and put a basic outline sketch on it. From time to time look at it, as you work on the bird. This can help to firm up ideas.

THOUGHTS ON BASES (Fig 193)

It is appropriate at this point to digress from the sequence of work for a moment or two, and to look at how the design of a base can alter the look of the subject. Whilst, in this project, the bird, leaves and branches each have an equal part to play in the overall design, this is not always the case. Sometimes you may wish to focus only on the subject. It is then necessary to use a base which has quite a different shape to the general form of the carving – square or oblong for a rounded subject will visually divorce the two, for instance. At other times, separation can be created if the subject is lifted high above the base, by the use of a metal rod or piece of wooden doweling.

Choosing the right shape can mean experimenting with different ideas; making trial bases out of softwood off-cuts for cheapness.

FINAL WORK ON THE BIRD

The jobs left to do were things like sanding – I opted for a smooth bird – final shaping of the beak, and carving the eyes, using the ¼in (6mm) No. 9 gouge to form their outline. The tail was left plain, without feather lines, as there were attractive natural bands. None of these things should present any great problem, since they are all closely related to work done in earlier projects.

Before it could be mounted, the bird had to be separated from its temporary mounting block. I did this by taking small cuts, to ensure that the underside did not become too flat. After separation, further work on the bottom meant that the carving had to be held in the bench vice, using kitchen sponges as pads to prevent any crushing of the wood. I had to take care to avoid applying too much pressure with the tools.

Fig 192 Start thinking about the base early on.

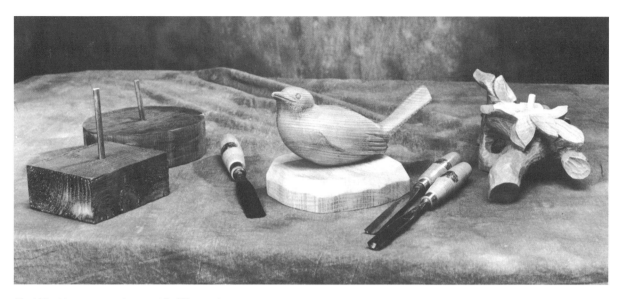

Fig 193   You can experiment with different shapes.

MOUNTING THE BIRD (Figs 194–197)

As mentioned previously, the design of the base is a matter of personal interpretation. The photographs alone should provide a guide to the combination of leaves and branches. The essential thing is not to get it all too flat. Use what you learnt about carving in relief to achieve plenty of contour variation to the shape. You will need to use wood at least 4in (100mm) thick and of a similar width.

Although I worked the base to a rough sketch, after the initial saw cutting I let much of the shape evolve as I carved it, by simply following the figure patterns in the wood. This helped to give a better 'flow' to the design than if it had been worked to a preconceived and detailed drawing.

In order that it can be gripped in the vice, it is well worth having at least two parts of the base left long and strong. Cut them back later when the carving is complete. Individual shapes of leaves were made by using mainly the ³/₄in (20mm) No. 3 and No. 4, and the ¹/₂in (13mm) Nos. 7 and 9 gouges. Incidentally, a hole in the base, drilled and then opened out using the No. 9 gouge, creates a sense of lightness, which will overcome a heavy, or cumbersome, look.

Whilst gouges can be used, inverted, to form the branches, and the No. 2 skew chisel is useful too, some of the work may need to be carried out with a

rasp, or with coarse sanding paper, in order to get a more evenly rounded shape. For accurate work, you will need to use two centre lines: one drawn on the side of the branch and the other on the top. To plot how they twist, or pass behind one another, use coloured chalk.

When you come to the final modelling process, a couple of points are worth bearing in mind. Firstly, you definitely need to know the type of finishing treatment you will give to the leaves and branches. Because I had decided to keep the bird smooth, I needed to add contrast. I gave the branches a textured finish by making small gouge cuts similar to those used in the mirror carving. For additional emphasis, I sanded the leaves a little, but not enough to make them as smooth as the bird. I decided that leaf veins were not necessary, because of the figuring of the wood. However, I did draw up the middle of some leaves to a ridge, to produce better light reflection. This was done using the fishtail No. 3 and the No. 6 longpod.

Secondly, when you come to cleaning up the work to get rid of stray fibres and any unwanted marks, there is quite a considerable surface area to work (when you take into account all the nooks and crannies, the underside of the base, and the edges of the leaves), so it is best to be very methodical. Rather than jumping around from one part to another, work

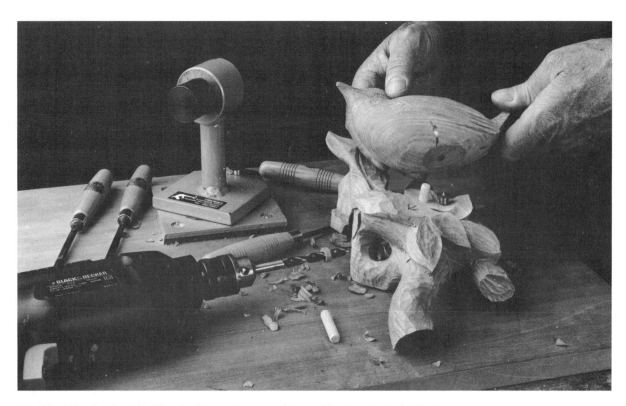

Fig 194   Using the dowel kit. Note the lines and arrow marking to aid re-locating the bird in the same position after removal.

Fig 195   Take time to make sure the position is right. Dowel, cap and drill with depth gauge shown.

a small area, finish it completely, then move on. This way you are less likely to miss rough areas, and it is quicker too.

The small, flat part of the underside of the bird's body has to nestle comfortably in the cushion of leaves. This requires persistent checking as wood is pared away from the base – *you should not have to alter the bird at all.* Although you can offer up the bird and lightly score round the underside, you may need a template to help you judge where wood has to be removed from. If you find it at all difficult to cut a card to the required shape, try pressing the bird into a slice of soft white bread. The flattened part will give you the shape you need, and you can just trim off the excess.

When testing for size, it is essential that the bird is always facing the same way each time it goes back onto the base. Make suitable pencil lines on both body and base as guides. When the seating seems reasonable, be content to leave it well alone. Persistently trying to 'improve' matters always seems to make them worse.

I joined the bird and the base together using a ¼in (6mm) diameter dowel, 1½in (40mm) long.

If you buy a dowel kit, you will get all the things you will need: dowels, the correct size of drill, and a depth gauge to prevent you from drilling too deep. You should also have in the kit a pointed dowel-cap. This fits into the first hole you make and gives you the exact mating position for the second hole. These caps are invaluable, and are far better than trying to get the location right with a double-pointed nail.

Before I fixed the two parts together permanently, I gave both the base and the bird a couple of coats of sanding sealer, except for the areas to be glued, which were left untouched. When it had hardened, each coat was sanded lightly with 500 grit paper.

The base and the bird were assembled dry just to check once more that everything was as it should be and that no further work was required. Gluing was carried out using 'Cascamite' wood adhesive with the bird and base clamped together.

Fig 196   Dowel cap.

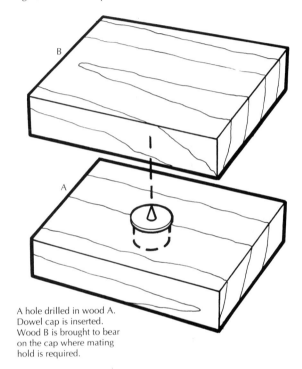

A hole drilled in wood A. Dowel cap is inserted. Wood B is brought to bear on the cap where mating hold is required.

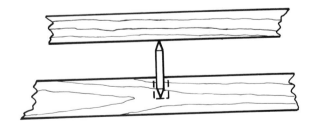

A nail pointed at both ends can be used but is less effective.

Fig 197   Dowel cap in use; better than a double-pointed nail.

Fig 198   Now you are ready to fly solo!

Glossary

Allongee Carving tool with a blade which tapers to the handle.

Arkansas stone Oilstone made from natural stone (US origin).

Back-bent spoon Gouge with a reverse-bent blade.

Bandsaw Powered saw with a continuous blade.

Bevel Part of blade ground to form a cutting edge.

Bowing Distortion of planks and boards, generally to the width, caused by imperfect drying, stress or shrinkage. This is the opposite of cupping.

Burr Rough edge produced when sharpening a tool.

Carver's mallet Used for striking gouges. Has a round head. Usually made from Beech, or from Lignum vitae wood.

Chisel Flat-bladed cutting tool.

Coping saw Handsaw which uses narrow, disposable blades. Suitable for sawing curves.

Cupping Distortion of a plank or board across its width.

Endgrain Surfaces showing cell ends.

Feather edging An edge tapered to appear thinner than it really is.

Fishtail Gouge or chisel with a blade that is wider than its shaft and that tapers steeply.

Gouge Basic carver's tool. Has a curved cutting edge, which distinguishes it from a chisel.

Hardwood Technical term for timber from broad-leaved trees.

Heartwood Prime carving wood, from the part of the tree between the sapwood and the central pith.

Honing Act of sharpening using an oilstone, or mechanically, using abrasive compound.

Incised carving Design cut into the surface of the wood using a V-tool or veiner.

India oilstone Man-made oilstone.

Paring Wafer-thin cuts.

Rasp Type of file used specifically for wood.

Riffler Miniature file, usually shaped or curved.

Ripple cuts A series of shallow, undulating cuts made on the surface of the wood, especially used as background treatment.

Roughing out Creating a basic outline, often with use of broad cutting tools.

Sap Tree's food in solution.

Sapwood The living area lying between the bark and the heartwood.

Seasoning Drying time to remove sap and moisture.

Slipstone Small, shaped oilstone, used to remove burr from the inside edge of a gouge.

Spokeshave Hand-held plane with two handles, useful for making cylindrical shapes.

Strop Leather strip, coated with polishing paste, used to improve the sharpness of a cutting tool.

Surform Proprietary rasp.

Sweep The curve of a gouge blade's cutting edge.

Undercut To cut back below the surface of a design at an angle.

V-tool Tool with two chisel-like blades set at an angle to form a V.

Veiner U-shaped gouge used to make decorative cuts.

Warping Distortion caused as timber dries. (*See* Cupping and Bowing.)

Workholder Purpose-made carving clamp.

Specific Gravities

It is useful to know the specific gravity of a particular species of timber, as it provides a guide to the wood's density. Generally speaking, the density gives the indication of how the wood may carve. For example, a high density wood is more likely to need greater effort on the part of the carver than one of low density. However, as far as overall carving quality is concerned, the density factor should only be used as an approximate guide. There are other aspects of the make-up of timber which should be taken into account. These will include: how dry the piece of wood is; the colour and disposition of any figuring; cell bonding; run of grain. An experienced carver would take all these factors into consideration. But of these density is unlikely to be far from the top of the list.

Specific gravity (SG) is the ratio of weight of any substance to the weight of an equal volume of water, at the same temperature. For accuracy, the wood to be measured must have a known moisture content; usually this is 12 per cent.

The majority of woods have a specific gravity less than the SG factor of 1.00, which means they will float when immersed in water. But there are a few very heavy, dense, woods with a greater SG factor (more than 1.00), which sink when placed in water. Ebony is a typical example – its specific gravity is 1.03. Another is African Leadwood, rated at SG 1.30. Most timber suppliers include SG figures when describing woods, but the following examples may prove useful.

Specific Gravity (SG) of Some Popular Carving Woods

Ash	0.71
Beech	0.72
Cherry	0.61
Elm	0.55–0.58
Lime	0.54
Oak	0.67
Sweet Chestnut	0.54
Sycamore	0.61
Walnut	0.64

APPENDIX 2

Abbreviations Used in Trade Classification

Timber merchants are liable to resort to abbreviated descriptions when listing timber. They also have their own forms of classification. You may find the following expressions useful to know when you visit wood yards to buy your carving wood. They are in use throughout most of the world.

A/D Air Dried. This describes the method of seasoning. The wood is stacked out of doors, allowing fresh air to circulate. It takes about one year for each inch (25mm) of thickness for the moisture content to reduce to that equal to the amount of moisture in the air. Generally better carving wood is produced by air drying. (The alternative method – kiln drying – is listed under 'K/D'). It should be noted that after seasoning the moisture content in the wood will still be higher than that of a centrally heated house, so further, careful, drying in the workshop will be necessary.

Billets Small round logs.

Conversions Term used to describe the process of sawing logs into boards.

End reared or **End racked** Timber stacked on end after having been sawn into boards or lengths, to preserve the natural light colour of the wood. This treatment is generally confined to woods such as Lime and especially to Sycamore.

F/S Freshly sawn (may not be dry).

K/D Kiln dried. The method used to dry wood in controlled conditions by careful adjustment of the temperature. An alternative method is to use a flow of ultra-dry air. Kiln drying is more accurate than air drying as the moisture content can be reduced to as low as 12 per cent, although 12.5–15 per cent is

average. Often A/D wood is finished off by kiln drying. NOTE: Kiln drying is not so successful where the thickness of the wood is greater than $2^{1}/_{2}$in (64mm), as internal splits – called shakes – can occur.

P.A.R. Planed all round.
P/S Partially seasoned.

RE Rare and exotic.

1S/E One square edge. Boards which have wane (where the bark grew) and sapwood on one edge, but sawn square on the other.
SG Specific gravity.
Shakes Internal splits – not visible until the wood is cut. They can be the result of kiln drying, bad felling by allowing the tree to fall heavily, or by strong winds.
Surfaced Indicates that all or part of one face of a board has been planed or sanded to reveal the figuring (grain) and colour.

T/T Through and through. The process of converting logs into boards by sawing the logs through their length any given number of times depending on the required thickness of each board. The boards then have wane and sapwood on either side, and the heartwood in the middle.

Wane The outermost part of a board corresponding to where the bark would have been.

APPENDIX 3

Metric Conversion Table

INCHES TO MILLIMETRES AND CENTRIMETRES						
MM = Millimetres CM = Centimetres						
INCHES	MM	CM	INCHES	CM	INCHES	CM
1/8	3	0.3	9	22.9	30	76.2
1/4	6	0.6	10	25.4	31	78.7
3/8	10	1.0	11	27.9	32	81.3
1/2	13	1.3	12	30.5	33	83.8
5/8	16	1.6	13	33.0	34	86.4
3/4	19	1.9	14	35.6	35	88.9
7/8	22	2.2	15	38.1	36	91.4
1	25	2.5	16	40.6	37	94.0
1 1/4	32	3.2	17	43.2	38	96.5
1 1/2	38	3.8	18	45.7	39	99.1
1 3/4	44	4.4	19	48.3	40	101.6
2	51	5.1	20	50.8	41	104.1
2 1/2	64	6.4	21	53.3	42	106.7
3	76	7.6	22	55.9	43	109.2
3 1/2	89	8.9	23	58.4	44	111.8
4	102	10.2	24	61.0	45	114.3
4 1/2	114	11.4	25	63.5	46	116.8
5	127	12.7	26	66.0	47	119.4
6	152	15.2	27	68.6	48	121.9
7	178	17.8	28	71.1	49	124.5
8	203	20.3	29	73.7	50	127.0

Index